Eardisley Characters & Capers

Eardisley Characters & Capers

by
Brian Hales
with
Susan King

Logaston Press

LOGASTON PRESS
Little Logaston Woonton Almeley
Herefordshire HR3 6QH

First published by Logaston Press 2005
Copyright © text Brian Hales 2005
Copyright © cartoons and map John Hawes
Copyright © photographs as acknowledged
and those villagers and friends whose pictures have been used

ISBN 1 904396 38 0

Set in Times and New Baskerville by Logaston Press
and printed in Great Britain by
The Cromwell Press, Trowbridge

*Front cover: Margaret and me on a Francis Barnet motorcycle at Modello Works
about 1946 or 1947. This is just how I remember Margaret looking when we played
together — with plaits and smart fawn dungarees.*

To Jason and Alexander

also to Elwyn 'Nick' and other late friends
to whom I'd have loved to give a copy of this book

Contents

page

Acknowledgements   *viii*

Foreword   *ix*

Introduction   *xi*

Location Map   *xii-xiii*

Chapter One: Early Days   1

Chapter Two: The War   11

Chapter Three: The Two Garages   33

Chapter Four: Motorcycles   45

Chapter Five: Pals   53

Chapter Six: Village Life   69

Chapter Seven: An Impressionable Age   93

Chapter Eight: Men Being Boys   109

Chapter Nine: Changes   119

Index   141

Acknowledgements

I should like to thank the very many people who have helped me with this book. First of all, my wife, Margaret, who has been there since I started and seen this book through with me. More people than I can possibly name individually have shared their memories of Eardisley with me — over a long period— but in recent times, while I have been writing, Brian Jones has given me particular support and encouragement. Malcolm Mason, of the Eardisley History Group, has been generous in his co-operation with my research and Sara Harris, also from the History Group, kick-started production of the book by typing the first draft. John Hawes used his skills as a cartoonist and a cartographer to help readers picture the stories I have written about. Nancy James photographed me — so readers can see on the back of the book what the young fellow on the front cover turned out like 60 years on. Ray Marsh scanned hundreds of photographs; Don Killick, Philip Wilson and Bill Griffiths also gave help. Lots of friends have been extremely generous in lending photographs; my thanks are also due to Brigadier Edward Tait, of the Museum of Army Flying, for permission to reproduce the three glider photographs on pages 27 and 28; to Liz Griffin, Editor of *The Hereford Times*, for permission to reproduce the photographs on pages 12, 85, 102 (top), 112, 128 (top), 122 (top), 131 and 136; to Ed McCartney of the First Engineer Special Brigade, 3939th Quartermaster's Gas Supply Company, U.S. Army for the pictures taken in 1943 on pages 13 and 15 (bottom); also to David Gorvett and the Eardisley Archive in Hereford Record Office for the above two photographs and those on pages 17, 18, 62 (along with Clive Davies), 101 (bottom), 102 (bottom), 105, 107 and 128 (bottom); to Eardisley WI for permission to reproduce photographs from their archives notably those on pages 21, 42, 69, 76, 82, 84, 98, 101 (top), 109, and 133; and to Ev Hatcher for that on page 77. Paul King made Sue and me lots of tea and coffee and always made me feel welcome. Andy Johnson of Logaston Press has made things easy for us and been enormously reassuring. In addition there are people too numerous to mention by name who have given me help and encouragement. But special thanks must go to my editor (and more), Sue King, who gave so much time and help in writing this book and whose kindness, patience and humour made it such a pleasure. She has been brilliant.

Foreword

I was very pleased to be asked to write a few words for Brian's book because I feel sure that among all the people mentioned I am probably unique. You see, I saw Brian when he was only a few hours old. We were neighbours then, and now, many years later, we are again neighbours.

I have no recollection of what this new baby looked like – I was only 12 at the time and much more interested in hockey than babies. Through the years I have many recollections of Brian and his family.

Gerald, Brian's father, and his sisters, Shirley and Margaret, were members of the Eardisley Dramatic Society with me, as were several members of his gang – Elwyn Nicholas, Brian Jones and Ronnie Barker, but only once did Brian 'tread the boards'. This was probably because he was not such an extrovert as the rest of us and we probably frightened him off acting for ever.

In 1946 Gerald drove me to Church for my wedding and in 1951 at 7.30 am he drove me to Hereford hospital when my son Andrew was born. Both these journeys were in the brown Austin 18 but they were very different. On the way to the wedding Gerald chatted happily, taking his time, because according to tradition brides should be a little late. In 1951 it was a different story – Gerald cheerfully remarked, 'We shan't have to hang about because I have to be back for the school run'. Unfortunately it was market day and on the outskirts of the city we got mixed up with a herd of cattle being taken to market. Nevertheless I reached hospital safely and I'm sure Gerald managed the school run.

I am so very fortunate having Margaret and Brian as neighbours because of the way they care for me. I look forward to reading Brian's book because I know that many of his memories will be mine and will recall for me many happy years spent in this super village of Eardisley.

Evelyn Hatcher

Introduction

1937 — the year I was born: life in Eardisley must have been very busy then, the village having its own self-supporting shops, all the different trades, characters of all sorts. My experiences as I grew up were mostly good as I recall over the years. Although the Second World War was starting, life went on as good as possible. Men were called up to the armed forces — some volunteered, women went as well. Others joined the ARP, Home Guard and other units such as the fire brigade and the police. Everyone did their bit for the country. Some men and women stayed to help with farming and mining and other essential tasks.

Country life during the war was not as bad as in the big cities; foodwise, we were able to get on quite well, being a farming community, and we were able to get vegetables and fruit as most people around here had large gardens and used them to feed their families. Although the community worked very hard and long — as they seemed to in those days — people had a good sense of humour and got on as best they could, helping and sharing with plenty of fun and friendship. Life appeared to me, as a young boy then, like an adventure into the future, which, looking back, I suppose it has been. I am sure there are other villages with their own stories and characters but Eardisley is where I have lived and enjoyed living and I think this is where I will rust out. Maybe this book will give a little something back to Eardisley for the good times we have had. I hope so.

Arboyne House 23
Ashcroft 34
bales of straw in the fields (where I
　　learnt to ride motorbikes) 66
Bank House 29
Bird's Pitch 1
blacksmith (Simon Ashby) 62
blacksmith (Tom Burgoyne) 28
bowling green at the rectory 59
Bridge House 39
cadets, purpose-built hut for 52
Cartref 22
Clematis Cottage 10
Cruck House 14
Dairy House 42
Doctor's bridge 36
Donkey's Corner 67
dump, Almeley road 46
dump, Chennels Gate 8
East View 42
Electric Sawmill 64
farms:
　　Parsonage 6
　　Powell's 42
　　Upper House 18
　　Wooton 5
Field, The 4
Folly, The 9
footbridge 54
Forester's Cottage 16
Gwatkin (home of the Miss Gwatkins) 25
Gypsy Hall 11
hiding place 57
High Gardens 15
Holme, The 26
Howells, Sam's wooden hut 63
Institute, The 31
Jones's garage 20
Jubilee bungalows 21
Kitty Darling's 3
Knapp House 12
laundry 33
Modello Works 30
Morgan's sawmills /Thames Timber 60
New Inn 19
Northway 13
Old Forge 17
police house 43
post office 44
railway carriages of Mr & Mrs 'Napper'
　　Davies 55

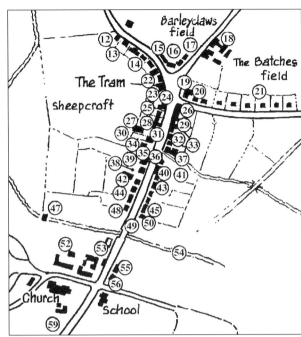

sawdust we rode our bikes into 51
Sharples' haulage 37
Sheep Dip brook and old pound 53
shops:
　　butcher's – 'Brierley's' 50
　　butcher's – 'Wynne's' 29
　　cobbler's – 'Dick Webb's' 24
　　electrician's – 'Charlie Carter's' 38
　　general – 'Davies the carriages' 55
　　general – 'Wilf Morgan's' 48
　　grocer's – 'Povey's shop' 23
　　grocer's – 'Triffitt's' 32
　　newsagent's – 'Clark's 40
　　newsagent's – 'Janet's' 29
Southway 60
stanks 37
stile beside a six-barred gate (wedding ropes) 53
Stoneleigh 35
surgery 44
Tennis Club 72
Townsend, Ken, house where he lived as a boy 49
Turn, The 7
village hall 28
waterfall 62
watermill house and waterwheel 51
White House, The 68
Wilkin, The 2

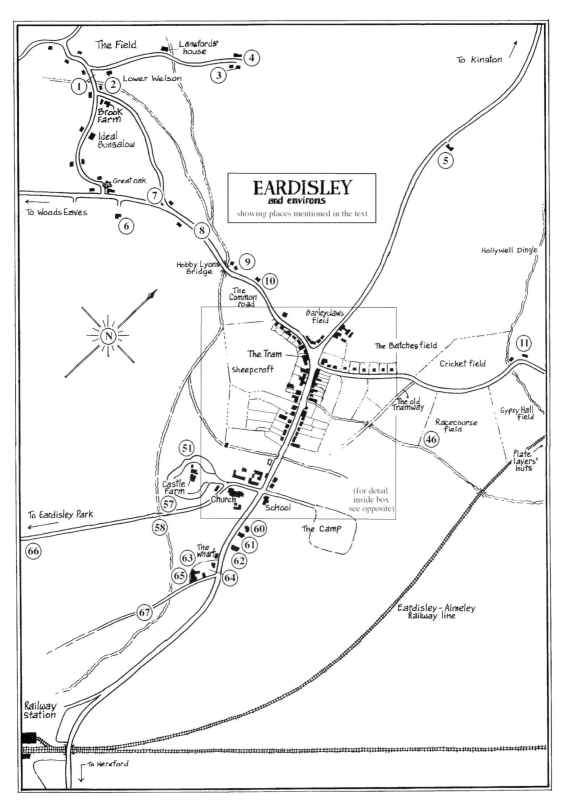

EARDISLEY
and environs

showing places mentioned in the text

The Field
Lansfords' house
Lower Welson
Brook Farm
Ideal Bungalow
Great oak
To Woods Eaves
To Kington
Hollywell Dingle
Hobby Lyons Bridge
The Common road
Barleyclaws field
The Tram
sheepcroft
The Batches field
Cricket field
The old Tramway
Racecourse field
Gypsy Hall field
Plate layers' Huts
Castle Farm
Church
School
The Camp
To Eardisley Park
The Wharf
(for detail inside box see opposite)
Eardisley-Almeley Railway line
Railway Station
To Hereford

Chapter One: Early Days

My parents were both born in 1908 and met in Eardisley, I think in the late 1920s. My mother, Clara Higgs, had come from Abersychan, near Pontypool to work for Mr Bob Wynne the butcher. She and my father, Gerald Hales, were married in Eardisley church in about 1930 and soon afterwards they went to live in London, where my father had a job with a car firm. (Harry Burgoyne told me that he asked my father to look for a job for him while he was in London. My father found Harry a job and as a result Harry worked in London for some time and got to know it very well.)

A few years later they, with my brother, John, who had been born 'within the sound of Bow bells' in 1932, returned to Eardisley and my father started work at Modello Garage, which was owned by Mr Richard Darling, son of the local doctor, Dr John Darling, who lived at Bridge House. My family went to live at The Wilkin, about a mile up the road from the village, and there my sister Shirley was born in 1935 and I was born in 1937. While the family was living at The Wilkin, Mr Darling decided to have a bungalow built for them close to Modello Works and when it was finished and I was about nine months old we moved in. The bungalow was given the name Ashcroft — presumably because of the ash trees nearby. (As I grew up I found these very useful, and I had a lot of fun swinging from their boughs and building tree houses in them.) A little later, in 1940, my sister Margaret was born. The four of us grew up, despite the war, in a very happy home.

My mother was a short, plumpish woman, who liked her home and liked a laugh. I remember her often being with the woman who delivered newspapers, Mrs 'Pecker' Davies, who would call in for a cup of tea and a chat. (I think 'Pecker' referred to this Mrs Davies's husband's nose, which was quite big.)

My brother was always into machinery and making things. At Christmas one year, when I was about five years old, I remember him giving me a little wooden tractor and trailer he had made for me, with wooden wheels, rubber tyres and wonderfully realistic towing hitches. My imagination worked overtime: in my mind I felled and carted away most of the timber around Eardisley, called into the garage for repairs and then got back to work delivering the timber.

Trip to Porthcawl, 1930s. Back, left to right: Mrs Leonard Hales (Ellen) — my granny
— and Miss Edith Brookes — Dick Brookes's sister.
Front, Mrs George Williams (Beatrice) and her sister Mrs Jack Brookes (Rosa)

Modello Works when it was owned by R O Darling.
In front, left to right: Fred Kite, Gerald Hales, Richard Darling

Clara Higgs, my mother, in the late 1920s

John sometimes milked the cows at Powell's farm (East View) and on one occasion he called me to go round to the milking parlour when he was doing this. The parlour had a split door to it and the top half was already open; I opened the bottom half and walked in, to be greeted by a faceful of warm milk! Big brother had scored a bulls-eye as he turned the cow's teats in the general direction of the door as I walked in. He thought that was a great joke. I didn't think much of it but one expects that sort of thing of big brothers.

It wasn't as bad as the time one Sunday morning when he took me to where the pigs were kept in the old barns (now Castle Close). Although I was already in my best Sunday clothes he persuaded me it would be a good idea for me to jump on the back of one of the biggest pigs and have a ride. I was all for doing this — not knowing my brother would help the pig off to a flying start! The pig left me behind in a foot of manure and I found this very difficult to explain to my mother when we got home: Sunday school was not usually as dirty and smelly as that. The problem was that if I said too much about what had happened I could not expect to get any more of big brother's cod-liver-oil-and-malt, which we both liked very much. John would buy a jar of this and hide it from me, as he knew I would have some of it without him knowing if I found it. Having a squirrel complex myself, I eventually found the cod-liver-oil-and-malt jar, half full and lying on its side, in the cab of an old lorry which had been in the bottom end of the bus shed for a long time. I don't think big

My brother, John, in a school photo outside Eardisley school in 1939. John is on the right, Michael Davies is in the middle and one of the teachers, Miss Ella Preece, is on the left.

brother realized how much was going from his jar, because he renewed it from time to time. It helped me to forgive him for the rough rides he sometimes gave me. But he was a good brother to me really, and, like my sisters, Shirley and Margaret, a good friend.

Shirley helped serve petrol at the garage from a young age, dressed the part in a fawn pair of overalls. She had her fair hair in long ringlets and was always smiling. Margaret, who I remember with plaits with bows at the end — and again, always smiling — also liked to wear fawn overalls and help at the pumps. Both Shirley and Margaret got on well with people and customers often enquired about how they were when they weren't there serving. Margaret enjoyed taking Mrs Josephine Burgoyne's baby daughter Lynn for walks in the village. Her time looking after Lynn seems a long time ago, but I'm sure it stood her in good stead for being a mother and a grandmother. She now lives with her husband David in Aberystwyth.

Next to the bungalow, a few yards away in the garden, were a couple of disused railway carriages. They had been there for years and long before my time a Bert Hughes had lived in them. During the war several families lived there at different times. Later my family used them as an extension to our bungalow — rather like a shed. I remember my mother boiling up the clothes in the carriages on washday. The carriages seemed to be quite comfort-able, with a fireplace and chimney and sleeping quarters. I remember the brass handles on the carriage doors, the thick leather straps to put the windows up and

Shirley and me in about 1941 outside Sunny Brook, the bungalow (now renamed Camilla Cottage) where my Hales grandparents lived for some time. My younger sister Margaret was possibly present when the photo was taken — inside the pram in the background. Looking at this picture reminds me of the shorts I was wearing — I remember that they were velvet and I particularly remember the feel of the little buttons (perhaps they were pearl buttons) visible just above my left knee. I have a few vivid memories of Sunny Brook — candles and oil lamps, a china dish to keep eggs in, with a lid shaped like a broody hen, and stuffed squirrels in a glass case. I also remember the lawn sloping down to the brook beside the lane. I played roly-poly down that slope; John used to roll Granny Hales's duck eggs down the bank and found it very funny if they bumped into something hard at the bottom and smashed.

down and the glass-covered map (above where the back of the seats used to be) showing the railway line, with the stops in colour. (I vaguely recall that the maps were of somewhere in the London area.) I found these carriages useful for a lot of purposes, from a boxing booth to a repair workshop. I also made several unsuccessful attempts at parachuting with an umbrella off the roof. The carriages, sadly, were eventually scrapped.

Modello Garage was ideally situated on the side of the main road. There were many buildings, of which the largest was used for parking private cars, post-office vans and other vehicles. R O Darling's, the business run from Modello Works, then comprised fuel sales, vehicle servicing and repair, a taxi service and a bus service, which, with its blue buses, was in competition with Midland Red. (I am told that the local lads at that time used to say 'Blue buses for ever, salmon tins for never' — but I am sure they were glad to see any bus for getting home.)

Mr Darling (usually known as Dick Darling) became quite a part of our family. A tall, slim man, quiet and well-dressed, he was a nice person who got on well with other people, though just occasionally, like most men at times, he could get annoyed when he was doing a fiddly job on an engine or if things

Bert Hughes outside the old railway carriages before Ashcroft bungalow was built at the back of Modello Works, 1930s. There were three sets of stationary carriages in or near Eardisley when I was young. The first I was aware of was in the garden of our bungalow, Ashcroft, at Modello Works, and when I was a little older I discovered Mr and Mrs Napper Davies's shop. The third is still to be seen set back from the road, just to the south of Eardisley, before the turning to Willersley. When I was young this carriage was the home of Bill Williams, who worked at the station — perhaps as a railway porter. I think it is now used as a summerhouse.

were not going well. Like his sister Kitty, he was willing to try new things. I have been told that their father, Dr Darling, was well liked in the village and I think I can visualize what he must have been like from what his son and daughter were like. In 1941 Mr Darling married Miss Alice May Smith, who had been a housemaid for the Darling household in Bridge House. My sister Shirley, who was then five and a half and who had been given the second name of May after 'Auntie May', was bridesmaid to her; I, then about four, was page boy.

Auntie May was a small-built person, always very neatly dressed. She often came round to our house and talked to my mother and to John, my sisters and me. I also remember going round on my own to see her in Bridge House. I remember reaching up to pull the long chain that rang the front door bell. (The front door was at the front of the house then, facing the road, which was about a foot lower then than it is now.) When the chain was pulled a line of bells along the passage started to ring and I was quite fascinated by this.

Wedding picture taken on the lawn at Bridge House, 1941. Back row, left to right: my father, Gerald Hales, Dick Darling and May Darling; Front: my sister Shirley and me

Auntie May used to take me into the sitting room, where there was a china cabinet with Queen Anne legs which impressed me. It had a glass top and sides to display a host of miniature china teapots, cups and saucers and much more. I do not know why this impressed me so much. I think maybe it was how neat and delicate it all was. It appeared to be a real work of art, so miniature and so well made (as a lot of things were in those days). I also thought how good it was of Auntie May to take the trouble to show me.

Three years later — on the 14th October 1944 — our family were on holiday in Wales when a telegraph boy brought us a telegram: Mr Darling had died suddenly. This was a huge shock to my parents as he was only 55 years old. We cut short our holiday and returned home immediately.

Me, about 8 years old

With my sisters, Shirley (left) and Margaret, outside Eardisley school in 1947 or 1948

This unforeseen tragedy brought about big changes in our life. My father, who was by now managing Modello Works, got together with the clerk, a Mr Ernie Crump, to talk about the future. Should they wait for someone else to buy the business or could they possibly raise the capital to buy it themselves? These were not easy decisions but they had to be made quickly and there had been no warning. Added to this was the fact that it was still war time and things were difficult. … He who hesitates is lost, they must have thought — but, on the other hand, fools rush in … The eventual outcome was that as partners they bought the business from May Darling.

Auntie May continued to live in the village, joining in activities such as the British Legion, WI and amateur dramatics, as well as bringing up Rosemary, the daughter she adopted after Mr Darling died. She died on 3rd May 1990, aged 95 years. Rosemary now lives in Hereford and has herself become quite a star in local dramatics.

Over the years I had quite a connexion with the Darling family, Dick, May and Kitty, but it is in later years that I have really got to realize and appreciate what wonderful people they were in my life and my family's. I am sure other people feel this too.

My father and Mr Crump carried on using the trading name of R O Darling, the premises continued to be called Modello Works and the business continued to a large extent unchanged, with Gerald Hales and Ernie Crump as joint proprietors. What had been the bus shed became a place where the people of Eardisley village garaged their vehicles, coming and going as they pleased with their cars — or sometimes their motorcycles or pushbikes. As I remember, a lady called Mrs Page, who rode a three-wheeled trike, used to leave it in the bus shed while she went off somewhere. My pals and I had great fun on the trike, up on two wheels, careering round and round the yard. Sometimes we would be lucky and someone would leave a motorcycle and sidecar; we found this a little more difficult on two wheels, but usually managed it somehow.

Four fuel pumps stood at the side of the main road. Originally the fuel was pumped by hand, by rotating a wheel on the front. When I was small — maybe about four — I once had a very nasty experience with the fuel pump. I swung on the operating handle, perhaps talking to Margaret or Shirley as I did so, not realizing the likely consequences of my action. Suddenly a huge amount of petrol poured down on my head like rain. At first I was completely over-whelmed by surprise and shock and then I began to feel a burning sensation wherever the petrol was touching my skin. I ran back to the bungalow and my

mother. Fortunately she was able to wash all the petrol off and I suffered no lasting ill effects. Not long after this, electrically operated pumps were installed.

The fuel wasn't just for cars: many places used some sort of engine which would probably run on paraffin or TVO (tractor vaporizing oil). An engine often used then was one called a donkey-engine, which was used for all kinds of jobs, often for driving electricity generators. We had one for this purpose at Modello Works. The engine was at the rear of the garage next to the battery shed (so called because it was where the batteries were charged). It seemed quite large to me then, with its two flywheels, one on each side. It was started with a handle, which you turned until there was a sort of chuffing sound and the engine had started. Once going it chugged away nicely, maybe now and again misfiring. The smell of the fuel as the engine worked away lingers in my mind, and even now reminds me of those boyhood days at Modello Garage.

So I grew up with vehicles and engines and this gave me a good start for later life.

Ernie Crump as a young man, possibly in an ex-services rehabilitation workshop, about 1917

8

Ernie Crump

Ernie Crump had been brought up in the boys' home at The Holme (on the corner of the Almeley road — where Bobby and Lizzie Smith now live) and had lost his right arm in the First World War. After being invalided out from the army he learnt the trade of carpentry in rehabilitation. He went to live — perhaps as a lodger — at Clematis Cottage (in what was then called The Common Road, but is now usually called Woodseaves Road) with the two Miss Batts sisters, Fanny and Annie. Eventually, perhaps when the ladies died, he took over Clematis Cottage, where he lived until he went into Kingswood Hall in his old age. He died in 1979.

At some point the opportunity arose for him to become a clerk at Modello Works. He had of course had to learn to write with his left hand after losing the right arm and his handwriting was extremely good, educated and distinctive in style. And it was the same with everything: he overcame his physical problems with enthusiasm — he always looked immaculate in every detail and it amazed me how he achieved this: cuff-links, shoelaces, tie were always perfect, his shoes always shone, his clothes looked just pressed. As for his home and garden, they too reflected his character. The house was a little old-fashioned but comfort-

Ernie Crump talking to a passer-by outside Clematis Cottage before setting off for work, about 1965

able and beautifully cared for. Outside he had a real cottage garden with little narrow paths of compacted soil, some edged with stone tiles and some with low privet hedges. The raspberry canes were covered with high netting in a proper wooden framework with a netted entrance.

He rode a high bicycle — a 28" frame, I should think — and he used this to collect his milk from Miss Madeline Powell's dairy (then called East View, now called Dairy House) in a white enamel can. Returning to the bike, with the handle of the can in his left hand, he would grasp the handlebar with this same hand (of course) to mount the cycle. This would have been quite a difficult manoeuvre for anyone but to Ernie it had become normal and unremarkable.

He was a very good tennis player — I think he used to play in tournaments for the Eardisley Tennis Club — dressed immaculately, of course.

I don't actually know exactly how he lost his arm. Ernie himself told me that he lost his arm during a lull in the fighting when he was a gunner. He had received a cake from home in a parcel and was hoping to share it out with the rest of the crew. He was attempting to cut up the cake — with a bayonet, perhaps? — when he felt a thump and realized his right arm had been hit. But someone else — a lady who lived in the village for many years and was a friend of Ernie's, Lily Boyce, told me that she thought a mule had kicked him and the arm went septic and had to be amputated. Another story that came from Ernie himself was that his trilby hat blew underneath a stationary Midland Red bus and whilst he was reaching to retrieve it the bus pulled away and drove over his arm. I don't think the bus story is very likely to be true but it was typical of Ernie to make light of things rather than suggest he was a war hero.

Gerald Hales clearing snow outside Modello Works 1963

Chapter Two: The War

During the war Lord Haw Haw, a propagandist for the Germans, reported that the people were so hungry that they were having to eat foxes. On hearing this, Mr Robert Wynne, Mr John Preece and Mr George Pritchard decided they'd show him. They held what they called the Fox Supper: Mr Wynne, the butcher, made a huge pie stuffed with so-called fox meat and a large number of people gathered together in the top room at The Tram. The pie, decorated with a fox mask and brush, was brought to the table to a fanfare blown on the hunting horn by John Preece, whose father and mother were landlords at The Sun Inn, Winforton. After a few words everyone settled down to a very enjoyable meal and a grand evening. I have never been able to find out what went into the making of the fox pie but there was very little of it left by the end of the evening — and not a lot of beer either. In 1959 a second Fox Supper was held and for this occasion the pie was once again made by Mr Bob Wynne (I think he was the only person to know all the ingredients). I often think how nice it would be if maybe one day we could revive the supper — for old times' sake.

Before the mills were extended, there was a lane by Eardisley school that led down to the Eardisley Camp. At the time that the camp was built — about 1942 — the railway lines were extended to the camp to bring in supplies. Later, Nissen huts were constructed, water and sewerage systems were laid on and the camp was ready for use as a very large fuel base.

We often used to go down to the camp and talk with the American soldiers, who were very good to us. Sometimes they would throw us chewing gum when we called to them as they drove through the village back to camp, after filling up their lorries with fuel from a pump at Mr Jones's garage, where they had their own supply. (Although the camp had ample stocks of petrol, it was stored for specific military purposes, and so, routinely, the lorries and other vehicles came from the camp to refuel at Mr Jones's garage.) Mud from the camp used to be brought through the village on the wheels or tracks of the vehicles, which left a lot of mess, but this could not be avoided as the camp was a very wet and muddy area and had little hard ground. I remember the Americans at the camp giving a party for the children of Eardisley school (which I was then 'mostly' attending). When they came to pick us up from the school to go down

John Preece blows the hunting horn for Mrs Phyllis Parker, landlady at The Tram, as she brings in the fox pie for the 1959 Fox Supper.

Mrs Phyllis Parker places the fox pie on the table. I cannot identify all the people, but seated on the far side of the table are, left to right, Mr Harold Davies, Mr George Pritchard, Mr Robert Wynne, Mr Sam Preece, Dr Edward Smythe and Mr Herbert Parry, and on this side of the table, (pictured side view), my school friend Edward Parry.

to the camp they had to put boards down for us, both to get into the lorries from the school and to into the huts at the camp, as the mud was so thick. At the party everyone was given a present of some sort and the food was really good. I always remember the fruit we had out of mess tins. After the party they took us for a ride up to The Great Oak — it was all very exciting.

After the Americans left the camp it became a POW camp for Italians and Germans. Most of the prisoners were all right and were able to go out and work among the local people, though I remember they had a large yellow spot, as big as a dinner plate, marked on the back of their shirts, so everyone knew that they were POWs. Often they worked very hard and enjoyed the relaxed freedom they had. My Uncle Jack Hales knew a lot of them quite well because he had a job driving them out to local farms in the morning to work, and collecting them again in the evening. Some were very clever, making rings and brooches out of threepenny bits. That seems a long time ago now but I can still see some of those characters in my mind, especially the ones who joined in with the locals skating on the moat at the castle in the moonlight. Some prisoners stayed after the war and settled down in and around Eardisley.

Mr Isaac Tauber was a Polish Jew, so I have been told, who came to Eardisley in the early years of the war. When he arrived in this country after leaving Danzig (like so many others) he was treated as an enemy alien and sent to The Isle of Wight for assessment. Eventually he was offered the opportunity to

Early days at the American camp — about 1942 — while it was still being constructed, looking north. After the war these huts were not all demolished straight-away. After the war, my Auntie Phyllis and Uncle Jack Hales lived for at least a couple of years in one of the huts you can see in the distance in this picture, as did the family of David Hamer and his wife.

13

manage a timber mill in Eardisley belonging to Mr George Morgan, which was situated next to Eardisley school, opposite the rectory. Soon after he began working at the sawmill he was joined by his family, his wife, his son, Edwin, and his daughter, Irene. (I particularly remember Irene as she was a friend of mine; she played the piano very well and practised nearly every day. I also remember that she loved to ride horses and she and I rode together for a few years — I always tried to make sure I rode my favourite pony, a lovely Welsh cob called Prince.) After the war the mill was extended to the old Eardisley camp where the Americans had been stationed; it was developed and modernized and became a very big business. At first called Thames Timber and later Parker Kislingbury, and dealing mainly with hardwood, it employed a lot of people from Eardisley and around for many years. Although Mr Tauber died while still quite young, his widow and Edwin and Irene carried on the business for some time afterwards. Today there is no longer a sawmill there but another timber firm — Forest Fencing — has taken over the site.

Ken Townsend worked most of his life in the sawmills Mr Tauber ran, mainly as a saw-doctor, and later as a machine operator until he retired. Ken was very clever at making things, as can be seen around his home at Forester's Cottage,

Bernard Jones at the fuel pump in the forecourt of Oliver Jones's garage in the Almeley road, 1950s. This was the fuel station the Americans at the camp had used during the war. It was because the Americans drove their lorries from the extremely muddy camp at the bottom of the village, all the way along Church Road and round into the Almeley road, to get petrol here that they caused the road to be so dreadfully muddy — 6" deep in places — through the village.

The Barley Field, Eardisley — me behind Robert Whittall (Elsie Whittall's son) on my favourite pony, Prince, (actually he belonged to Irene Tauber) — about 1949

which is marked out by the weather vane of Tom and Jerry situated at the top of the chimney.

As a boy he lived by Mr Brierley's butcher's shop (in the house Mrs Margaret Fitness now lives in). He went to the village school and used to sing in the church choir (as did his mother, who also had a good voice). Often he was sent over from the school to sing in the choir for a funeral. When Ken was quite young he also did many duties in the church, such as lighting and stoking the stoves; sometimes he pumped the air for the church organ if the organist wanted to practise — he was paid 6d for this job. At that time there was an organist who had come down from London because of the bombing and stayed at the rectory. He was used to playing big organs in cathedrals and Ken found it very hard work keeping enough air pumped to the organ — he definitely earned his 6d when he was pumping for him!

Fuel supplies coming to the American camp in the early 1940s. The lorries are up to their axles in the mud — you can imagine what this mud did to the roads in Eardisley village.

During the war, as it was blackout Ken would take a torch to the church to stoke the fires or check on them for evening service or other functions. On one occasion when he came out of the church he switched on his torch and the bulb blew so he was left completely in the dark. Being a young boy — about twelve or fourteen — he had difficulty finding his way out through the church-yard and the gravestones back to the main road — no street lighting then. *Not* the best situation to find oneself in, as Ken found out!

Ken was a clever man and often helped people out with little jobs. We miss him around as — sadly — he died at the age of 76 in 2004.

As lads, during the war it was a great thing for us to follow the training of the Home Guard and the ARP (Air-raid Precautions). The Home Guard would often parade on Tram Square, usually on Sunday mornings after church. The bugle would be blown by Sergeant Carter, an electrician whose shop was in the middle of the village and who later also had a shop in Hay-on-Wye. Charlie Carter was a big man with a ginger-ish look — a pleasant person. He wasn't at all the sergeant type as people think of it — a bit more of the Eardisley laid-back sort. They'd all be in khaki uniforms — prickly material — with their stripes on both sleeves, one stripe for lance-corporal, two stripes for corporal and three stripes for sergeant. Eardisley didn't have a sergeant-major as far as I know, but that would have been a crown on the forearm as well as the three stripes. Walter Howells was the captain, with three pips on the shoulder. The unit's medical officer also had the rank of captain and in Eardisley this was the local GP, Dr Miller.

Once, my pal Nowt (Brian Jones) and I were used as casualties, bound up with bandages and splints, and carried off on stretchers to some point down the road. This was great fun for us and we spent most of the journey laughing. I remember one exercise in which James Morris from The Folly had been 'volun-teered' to take the part of The Enemy. He had a band round his head (almost like an Apache Indian, not much like a German!) and mud on his face as though he'd been roughing it for a few days. He was obviously told in advance to go and hide in a particular area and then the members of the Home Guard were ordered to go and seek him out and capture him. About twenty-four 'soldiers' set off up the Almeley road, with rifles at the ready, in single file — with three little followers, me, Nowt and Nick (Elwyn Nicholas), excitedly bringing up the rear). When they reached the map reference they'd been given they turned left into The Batches field, spreading out to the perimeter of the field and heading towards Hollywell Dingle. After a short time there was a cry of 'Prisoner!' — which excited us even further — and we saw Jim coming out of a hollow tree with his hands in the air in the proper way. He was jokingly prodded with the Lee Enfield 303s and marched off — probably straight to the pub!

The ARP organized exercises to prepare civilians for what to do in various circumstances. I remember that one exercise involved bags being dispersed over an area, little dark blue cloth bags filled with something like sand and tied up with string at the top — they were acting as incendiary bombs. The idea was to learn the procedure should the real thing ever be dropped in Eardisley. The ARP used to wear a black or blue-ish uniform, I think, and steel helmets with a wide strap under the chin. They had gas masks which they carried in canvas satchels across their chests (though some ARP people just had their gas mask in a cardboard box on a sash or even just a piece of string).

Richard Brookes (father of Dorothy Joseph and Doreen Payne), who ran a coal business before Howells and Jones started up, was a member of the ARP. He was on duty the night a bomb was dropped on Cwmma Moors, just north of the village.

Another person active in the ARP was a Mrs Blanchard, who had two sons, Pikey (I don't know what his proper name was), and an older boy, and a

Eardisley Home Guard outside The New Inn in the 1940s.
Left to right, back row, Gwyn Stephens, Bill Bounds, Sam Mifflin, Owen Williams, Fred Kite, George Evans, ?, Jack Bowen, ?.
Second row, Evan Dyke, Percy, known as 'Barclay', I think because he was always talking about money, Davies (of whom it was said, but I don't know how reliably, that he either swam or paddled in a beer barrel from The New Inn to The Tram some time when Eardisley was flooded before the great floods of 1959), Sid Jones, Lewis Price, Walter Davies, Bert Davies, John Morris, Jack Jones, Frank Morgan.
Third row, Corporal Jack Prideaux, Lance Corporal Gerald Hales (my father), Edgar Morgan, Lance Corporal Wilfred Morgan, Captain Walter Howells, Sergeant Charlie Carter, Charlie Davies, Harry Bromage, ?, Ronald Taylor.
Front row, Tom Bengry, Charlie Jenkins, Corporal Oliver Jones, Jack Langford, Godfrey Skyrme, ?, Sergeant Reg Jones, Ernie, known as 'Child', Davies (who used to smoke cigarettes using a long cigarette holder)

Miss Edith Brown in her Land Army uniform in about 1945. Edith arrived in Eardisley from up north at the age of 17 on Armistice Day in 1945. She was to stay for a short time to work as a Land Girl for Miss Madeline Powell at East View in the middle of the village. But sixty years later she is still here. After arriving and settling down she was soon into the swing of things in the village. She worked hard, doing a daily milk round for many years, and was very popular as she took part in a lot of village life, helping to run the youth club and the tennis club, taking part in amateur dramatics, and helping to organize trips for the over-sixties, which meant a lot to the local people. Edith played quite a lot of sport then and although she has been retired for some time now she still enjoys playing golf today. I have known Edith since she arrived in the village and have always admired her enthusiasm for village life. I am sure others enjoy her company. She now lives at the top end of the village, sharing her home with Miss Kathleen Wolsey, who came to Eardisley in 1972 from Longtown, where she served as a district nurse for 23 years. Another wonderful character, still taking her walks in the village and a pleasure to talk with, at the age of 90 Miss Wolsey has just joined the over-sixties club!

Miss Edith Brown at work as a Land Girl

daughter, Ann. I don't know if there was a Mr Blanchard — maybe he was away in the war. For a short time their home was in the railway carriages at Modello Works; later they lived at The White House on the south side of where the fire station is now. Mrs Blanchard, as I recall, was a tall, slim lady, quite smartly dressed and well made-up — fairly well educated, I think, and nicely spoken. Pikey was about my age and was often about with Nick, Nowt and me. I remember going to his home at The White House and seeing a big net on a stick and wondering what it was for. Later I asked, and Pikey showed us a display case full of different sorts of butterflies, all neatly labelled. I don't think he had collected the butterflies himself; I think it was his family — his brother or his father perhaps. At the time — I was about six — I didn't think about how the butterflies came to be pinned inside the display case, I just marvelled at their colouring, shape and markings. I still have a clear picture of the scene outside the front door of The White House: Pikey, holding the case, and Elwyn and me, and perhaps Nowt as well, peering in admiringly.

Three generations of Powells, early in the 1940s: on the left, the current David Powell from Dairy House with his grandfather, David Powell; on the right, Percy Powell, father of the small boy in the picture and of the baby he is holding, Margaret Powell. A few years after this picture was taken I remember old Mr David Powell sitting on the carrier of the brown Vauxhall car inside the garage at the farm, looking out at the people going by. He would often call out to one or other of us going home from school to get him some cigarettes. We would go to the shop for him and buy the cigarettes and then go and have a chat with him.

School days 1942–1949

One day, while my mother was doing the washing in the railway carriage she saw the teacher walking down the road to the school. She quickly turned to me and said 'Would you like to go to school?' I thought for a moment and then replied that I would. So my school days began. The school building was basically the same as it is now but the windows on the west side were much higher then, so we could not see out. I expect this was to keep our attention on what was going on in the classroom but it made us feel rather like prisoners and after the first few days I only kept going under some duress.

The war was at a serious stage, but being very young we did not generally realize this even when we were practising the drill with our gas-masks and learning how to clean them. Off we went to school with the masks in little square cardboard boxes hung with a cord round our necks. Sometimes in the newspapers there was a small map of how the war was going and, as the Germans took more ground, more areas would be shaded with black. Even at that age we sensed how worried the grown-ups were as black started to cover more and more of the map. It was very exciting, though, as the reverse began to happen and eventually victory came.

The headmaster, Mr Ernest Bateson (we always *privately* called him Spud Bateson) was a small, thin, clean-shaven man. He smoked a pipe and, outdoors, usually wore a trilby hat. He had a stern manner in class that I found quite frightening. I remember having a lesson that was something like Technical Drawing in which he showed us how to use a set square. We were very young — I don't think more than seven. Mr Bateson had shown us just once how to use the instrument and I had not quite got the idea. He walked round the class, looking over children's shoulders and watching them. When he stood behind me I nervously attempted to work out what I was meant to do with the thing and at my first try got it wrong. I knew I had got it wrong because I felt a clip on my ear. I tried again and quickly felt his sharp hand again. Eventually I got it 'right' — but it was quite by chance: I was thinking far too anxiously about that hand on my ear to be able give any attention to what the idea of the set square was. He was very strict about behaviour too and did not spare the rod

Eardisley school at the time I attended it — 1940s. Notice the school bell up on the roof top and the height of the bottom of the windows — designed to prevent our being able to get distracted by gazing out of the windows! (The bell is now in a different place and the windows have been lowered.)

— as I found out on a few occasions. Like many others I knew where the cane was kept, which was in some tall green cupboards, on the top left-hand shelf. The cane was approximately two foot long, $^3/_8''$ thick and very strong — as my mate Nowt and I discovered while waiting for twenty minutes to be caned. We had been eating apples on our way back to school after dinner and as we passed Mr and Mrs Charlie Carter's house saw an upstairs window wide open. On an impulse we decided to see if either of us could throw an apple core straight through the window. Unfortunately for us, this was witnessed by a lady living opposite, Miss Parry (who lived where Malcolm and Theresa Mason now live).

When, a few minutes later, Miss Parry saw the school mistress, Miss Stratton, come out of the door of the Carters' house (where she was a lodger) to go back to school, she lost no time in reporting to her what she had seen. Miss Stratton in turn reported us to Mr Bateson, and we duly found ourselves waiting what seemed like forever outside Mr Bateson's room for our punishment.

We had heard it said that if you rubbed horse-hair on your hands before you got the cane the cane would break. By chance, as we were waiting for Mr Bateson to come and deal with us we saw a horse's tail of sorts on a shelf. The school was practising at that time for a play that required a horse's tail (it must have been artificial) — perhaps for someone's costume. In our fear for what was in store for us we took the tail from the shelf and vigorously rubbed our

Mr Ernest Bateson ('Spud') in the late Forties after his retirement, in one of his more relaxed moods — on the bowling green with the old Atco lawnmower

hands with the horsehair. I'm afraid when the caning came we discovered there was no truth in what we'd been told. The cane did not break and I particularly remember the noise and the hurt that followed the cane as it came down on my small hand for the *second* time. Afterwards it was difficult to write as hands that had been caned usually shook for some time.

As I got older and moved up the classes, I settled down to what I now term 'compulsory free will' as I found that school had its moments, its ups as well as downs. The first time I saw a banana was at school. One of the boys, Ewart Prideaux, a little younger than me, had brought one to school which his brother Geoff, who was in the navy, had brought home. We were like bees round a jam pot, even tasting the inner skin. Then there were the times when we dropped carbide into the inkwells. It made a real mess and once it was wet it seemed to bubble on forever, overflowing into the desks and exercise books. Perhaps we should have got the cane, but I think we got away with that!

Towards the end of my time at Eardisley school I became friendly with a boy called Byron Thomas, who then lived at Forester's Cottage opposite the Methodist chapel. He and I once cut ourselves to become blood brothers — we had heard so much about this (probably from the films). We used our penknives to cut into our thumbs just enough to produce a couple of drops of blood and then rubbed the two cuts together. Sometimes Byron would come with me when I went to Wooton Farm, where Mr and Mrs V Stephens lived, as this was a favourite place for me to go and ride ponies. Byron didn't ride himself but he was useful as one of the horses was at least half-mule — he was stubborn and could get nasty at times. After I had caught the animal and eventually mounted him, I would enjoy a ride into the village, with Byron keeping him moving by walking behind with a very long hazel stick. As I rode I kept an eye on the mule's ears as any movements of these were a tell-tale sign of his next move. Byron seemed to enjoy walking behind with this big stick as we made our way down through the village. He never seemed to want to get on the mule with me — maybe that was just as well, as I think if he had the mule would have made quite a scene.

One day, while I was going into the field to catch him, the mule was like something possessed, coming towards me on his hind legs and pawing at the air with his front legs. The situation looked very dangerous and I decided to call it a day. I went back to my faithful Welsh cob (Irene Tauber's Prince) — a much better animal. Even he had his times now and again, though. Once, while I was grooming him, facing his rear and with my backside in the air, I suddenly felt a shock of pain and jumped up. He had turned round and sunk his teeth into my backside, leaving very distinguished teeth marks. I think he thought it was a good joke. I didn't think it was at all funny — but it was a lot better than being pawed to death by a mad mule!

Wartime experiences of some Eardisley people

I was born just before the war and lived through it, but was of course too young to understand much about it at the time, but over the years I have come to know about the war experiences of some people who later lived in Eardisley. One of these was Captain Bowen.

Although he lived just outside Eardisley, Captain Alfred Edward Bowen used to come to my father's garage in the village for motor repairs and fuel. As a young boy I didn't know much about him, apart from meeting him at the garage. Skip (as he was known) always appeared to be very quiet and gentle, steady in his ways and liked by everyone he met. Although of course I wouldn't have called him that then, I refer to him now as 'Skip' because I am sure he would have liked me to — he was that sort of man — just one of the boys, if you like. I think he drove a Morris Minor car then and if one got behind him it was no trouble to overtake — he always drove very steadily. One could be forgiven for thinking that Skip had never been anything out of the ordinary. But that would be far from the truth.

In 1965 I was privileged to be invited down to Skip's home, where he and his wife Muriel made me very welcome. After a while Skip called me through to what he called *his* little room. We sat down comfortably and he said to me, 'I'd like to show you something I think you will be interested in.' And it certainly *did* interest me — very much.

In the First World War Skip had joined the Royal Flying Corps (after lying about his age) and carried out many frightening duties. (I expect it was at this time that he acquired the nickname Skip from being the leader that

Captain Alfred Edward Bowen in about 1917

23

*'Hon. Lieutenant A. E. Bowen, late
R.F.C., diving feet foremost. The rigging
tapes are seen fully extended; the silk
body is in the act of issuing from the
container and the air is entering its
mouth.' The caption underneath one of
the press photographs of Skip Bowen
making his historic leap off Tower
Bridge, on Sunday 11th November 1917,
wearing a Guardian Angel parachute*

*'THRILLING PARACHUTE DESCENTS FROM THE TOWER BRIDGE. ——
A new parachute, intended for use from low altitudes, the invention of Mr. Everard
Calthrop, was tested from the highest span of the Tower Bridge. The parachutist about
30 feet before touching water.' Handwritten notes (probably made by Skip himself) in
the top right corner of a copy of the picture say: 'Unopened Parachute 16ft 1st Second,
48 ft 2nd ", 80 ft 3rd ". Landing Speed 15 ft per Second. Dropping rate 120 ft in 2
Seconds'. (It is not clear whether the " marks within the caption mean 'ditto' or repre-
sent an abbreviation for 'seconds'.)*

he truly was.) At that time pilots were not routinely issued with parachutes and there was a need to develop chutes for military purposes; in particular a model had to be designed for quick release to enable the parachutist to get out of danger. Skip did many test jumps with one of the early chutes then in use, Calthrop's Guardian Angel 150. He told me that while testing chutes he would jump from various altitudes — from aircraft that themselves seemed to me quite terrifying. The drill was that overalls filled to a weight equivalent to Skip's were harnessed to a chute and dropped first. If all went well with this test-drop Skip would jump himself. He would report on the performance of the chute and if necessary it would be modified.

As Lieutenant A E Bowen he made one jump that I believe stands as a low-altitude record to this day: he jumped from London's Tower Bridge on Sunday 11th November 1917. I think this was quite a risky thing to do. In telling me about it Skip joked 'It's a good job it was high tide!', but his daughter, Mary, told me recently that when he talked to her about that day he always recalled that just before he jumped he noticed a dead bird at his feet. I think Skip somehow felt that this was a bit of a bad omen. In spite of bad omens, however, the outcome was ok: the parachute performed as it was meant to and Skip was made up to Captain for his achievement — but he told me it would have been much better if he had had £200 and a bottle of Scotch. What a wonderful man!

All this — learning about Skip's past and seeing the pictures — was a real treasure and surprise to me as — at the age of 28 — I had finally done something I had longed to do. With a few friends I had founded Hereford Parachute Club. This had turned out to be a big success and Skip, knowing that I was into para-chuting, thought I would like to see more about the subject. I felt very humble after seeing and reading what Skip had done in his lifetime.

Later in life for a while Skip was landlord of The Boat Inn at Whitney, where he used to promote boxing tournaments and other sporting competitions. He finished his time before retirement selling fertilizers to local farmers and died at the age of 82 on 2nd November 1970. He was a gentleman to the end.

Captain Bowen had the unusual distinction of having a tame fox as a pet. This photo was probably taken in the 1950s or '60s.

Ann and Rodney Wood moved to Eardisley in September 1965 with three young children — Liz (six), Andy (four) and Steve (two). Rodney had volunteered for the Royal West Kents in 1942. In 1944 he trained as a parachutist and was posted to the Second Parachute Battalion on their return from Arnhem. The battalion was briefed for a drop on Denmark but this was cancelled when German resistance collapsed. Rodney was transferred to 7 Battalion and flew to India. The intention was to parachute into Malaya, but this plan was aborted with the Japanese surrender and the battalion went in seaborne, on landing craft. Rodney heard a few angry shots but never fired any. In 1946 he was posted to Palestine as Intelligence Sergeant to 7 Battalion, but acted as Company Sergeant Major while the regular NCOs took end-of-war leave. He took part in a number of cordon-and-search operations and arranged company picnics on the Sea of Galilee.

Sergeant Rodney Wood in his Second Parachute Battalion uniform in 1945

When he left, Rodney told me, the major said to him, 'Mr Wood, you've run my company like a holiday camp'. 'I thanked him,' Rodney said, 'but I am not sure he meant it as a compliment'.

In June 2004 an Eardisley man — Tom Carter — was amongst the veterans revisiting the Normandy beaches for the D-Day commemorations. My friend Brian Jones, who was, of course only about seven years old in 1944, went with him. Tom served in the war with the glider squadrons in the Oxf and Bucks (The Oxfordshire and Buckinghamshire Light Infantry). He does not say much about his wartime experiences but now and again he will tell me little stories that I feel I ought to write about.

Tom Carter celebrating his 75th birthday in 2002

Tom was called up in March 1942 and initially did about four months' training with the Duke of Cornwall's Light Infantry, barracked at Bodmin in Cornwall. After this he was drafted to the Somerset Light Infantry for a spell of square-bashing and 'moving barbed wire around' on the east coast (actually, putting up mock defences with the intention of diverting the attention of the Germans from the Channel, where action was really planned). In 1943 he joined the 6th Airlanding Brigade of the 6th Airborne Division, which consisted of three brigades of paratroopers. (There were actually only two divisions, the 1st and the 6th, but the second was called 'the 6th' to confuse the enemy.)

Tom's first operation was D-Day on 6th June 1944 and his team were to fly to Normandy in a Horsa carrying ten men, a Jeep and a 20-mm Polsten gun. Before boarding the glider, Tom made his own special mark on her, carving 'Kathleen' (his wife's name) on the outside. After being released from the towing plane they flew towards a field on a hillside with many other gliders already parked on it, and landed without a problem because D-Day had been kept absolutely secret — it was said that it was the best-kept secret of all time. They were all able to get out with their equipment, form up and set off on patrol with the Jeep and the gun.

They were not far from the Pegasus bridge and spent a few days in Ranville village before moving out to a more country area where they dug in for defence. The weather turned murky and they thought this might be just the

A Horsa glider — the type Tom Carter flew in when he went to Normandy and other battlefields. Gliders were used to make troop drops into enemy territory. The gliders were only made of fabric-covered plywood but the design made them very strong. There were two types: the Hamilcar, loaded by the nose, and the Horsa, loaded at the side. These unpowered aircraft were towed by 4-engine bombers to within a short distance of their destination; once released they could stay up for some time, to complete their journey on air currents. Tom Carter says that generally the crew hadn't a clue where they would end up once they had been released from the towing aircraft.

The Polsten gun (allegedly so named after its Polish designers and the Sten factory where it was made) weighed about 5 cwt; the wheels on which it was mounted for manoeuvring were folded underneath as stabilizers for action.

Soldiers boarding a glider. The maximum load was 30 men, including two pilots.

Inside the glider. You can see from this picture that the men travelled all ready for action whenever and wherever they landed.

time for Jerry to come over, as they were then strafing supplies as much as they could. Sure enough, in came about eight or ten planes trying to hit supplies and aircraft, though when it actually happened they were taken by surprise as they were trying to have a bite to eat. Tom had already put a magazine in the gun and taken the covers off, so he immediately took his place on the gun and started to fire at the planes. By this time the main ones had gone. But Tom, after following his tracer shells through, kept firing and the next thing he saw was one of the planes coming down in a ball of fire to a cheer from the group — that at least was one less — but there many more.

Tom had one of his lucky escapes at this time. The base was not far from a water supply — only about 100 yards. When Tom returned to base after going to the pump to get himself some water someone asked him to get *him* some. Tom went back to the pump but while he was away there was an explosion close by and when he returned to base the second time he found that the group had been hit with a shell or a mortar bomb. There were lots of injuries and several of the men had been killed.

A happier memory for Tom, amidst all this horror, is of George Formby coming with his wife Beryl to entertain the troops. The military authorities had warned the couple of the great danger they would be in, especially from mortar bombs, but George and Beryl insisted on going ahead with the planned concert. George Formby was the first ENSA [Entertainments National Service Association] recruit to perform for the troops after the Normandy invasion.

Tom and his comrades spent the next three to four months holding the left flank until the enemy retreated as far as the river Seine. 'Then', says Tom, 'after we reached the river, we came back to dear old Blighty, embarking on landing craft off Mulberry Harbour' [the massive floating harbour that had been towed to France from England for the D-Day landings].

Some time later and back home, Tom and his unit were reforming and getting ready for their next mission, which was scheduled to take place after a short Christmas leave. Some of the men began to disperse on hearing unofficially about the leave, but at the last minute, because the enemy had made a breakthrough, it was announced that they were to go to the Ardennes in Belgium. The leave was cancelled and a Jeep was taken out to bring them back. But the Jeep was involved in a crash and another vehicle had to be requisitioned to round everyone up. Eventually, however, all present and correct, they were able to cross the Channel to Calais in landing craft and undertake their mission. They spent about three months in Holland, and then, after taking off on improvised runways, flew back home to Bulford camp on Salisbury Plain.

The next thing was the invasion of Germany. They arrived at RAF Brize Norton in March 1945 to find rows of gliders each side of the runway in herringbone fashion, ready to take off in pairs and get a lot of troops airborne quickly. They boarded the men and equipment and waited for take-off. It was dawn and Tom was very apprehensive — as I suppose they all were.

They took off, towed by a 4-engine bomber, and flew to their destination, where their glider was released for its pilot to find a suitable landing area, this taking some time because of all the anti-aircraft and landing craft barricades the enemy had erected. Looking through the portholes, Tom could see ack-ack shells coming up all around, sometimes exploding very close, now and again hitting a glider, he remembers thinking 'Thank ***! They must be missing us because otherwise we would not be here to see them'. 'It was', he says, 'like hell let loose'.

(Tom later discovered that conditions were so difficult that about half the men in the division were killed in the course of this landing.) Flak was coming up and the air was filled with fire and smoke from the crashed planes. The crew in Tom's glider were understandably tense and nervous. Eventually a young Cockney fellow got up and made his way to the cockpit. 'For ***sake get this thing down somewhere!' he shouted. At this the pilot decided to take his chances through the posts 10 feet high and 1 foot thick and brought the glider quickly down but when the aircraft finally came to a halt it was wingless and severely damaged — tailplane and wheels completely smashed. Miraculously, Tom and the rest of the crew survived but the fuselage was so badly damaged they could not get into it and had to abandon their equipment. Then they went off to rendezvous with the rest of the brigade, making their way to the sound of gunfire. As they went, they picked up prisoners and wounded men and saw a great many dead troops — the memory of the dreadfully gory things they saw then, says Tom, is with him still. He spent the remaining months of his war service peacekeeping in Palestine and was demobbed in March 1946, very thankful to be in one piece after a good few narrow escapes. After the war and his move to Eardisley, however, his luck changed.

On 2nd March 1960 he and his family moved from Bosbury, where he had been a farm contractor, to a Council smallholding at Questmoor. In the years following the move three members of his family died at an early age: his sister in a road accident in Birmingham, his wife, Kathleen, through illness and his younger son, Mervyn, in a drowning accident at Whitney. Years on, Tom's family was struck by tragedy again, when his older son, Mel, died of a heart attack while riding in a motorcross race at Narberth, Haverfordwest, on Sunday 20th June 2004 — Fathers' Day. These tragedies must all have been extremely hard to take, but, the sort of man Mr Tom Carter is, he has seen it through, knows he has done his best and today still keeps his chin up with a smile.

Tom is now getting on in years but he still enjoys a drink or two and keeping people in fits of laughter about some of the silly tricks he and his friends have played on one another over the years.

One story involved a dead badger that Tom found on the road one night on Bromyard Downs. Tom put the badger in the boot of his car and brought it home to Questmoor Farm, I suppose to bury it. Then he thought of a better plan. He took the dead badger over the road and in the dark propped it up against the back door of his neighbour, Mrs Sheila Anning. In the morning, when Sheila opened the door — to her surprise and fright — the badger 'dropped in' to visit her! I think Sheila guessed who had put it there as she was very used to Tom's pranks — she was only just beginning to forgive him for sewing a 'garment' of hers to her clothes line!

There are many people in Eardisley who worked in factories during the war years, some in the ammunition factories, which was dangerous apart from the risk of enemy attack because there was always the chance of a sparked explo-

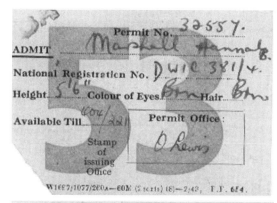

Permit No. 32557.

ADMIT Marshall Hannah B.

National Registration No. DWIC 3814.

Height 5'6" Colour of Eyes Brn Hair Brn

Available Till 604/21 Permit Office:

Stamp of issuing Office O Lewis

W1627/1077/280A—60M (2 serls) (8)—2/43. T.F. 6F4.

This permit is an Official Document issued and held subject to the provisions of the Explosives Act, 1875, and Official Secrets Acts, 1911-1939, and of the Defence Regulations, 1939.

Its unauthorised possession, use, retention, alteration, destruction or transfer to another person are penal offences.

The holder must produce this permit if required to do so by the Constabulary or other authorised person.

It must be returned to the Permit Office, if and when required, and in any case on expiry or when the holder ceases to hold the appointment or occupation on account of which the Permit was issued.

Signature
of Holder TO BE SIGNED IN INK

If found, this Permit must be hand-

GREAT WESTERN RAILWAY.

WORKMAN'S TICKET.

GREEN

No. 39 THIRD CLASS

AVAILABLE BETWEEN

PONTYPRIDD

AND

TREMAINS PLATFORM

Marshall H.E. Name of Holder

(BRIDGEND) R 32557 Identity Number

NOT TRANSFERABLE

Issued subject to the By-laws, Regulations, Notices and Conditions published in the Company's Bills and Notices.

Available for one return journey daily by authorised trains.

Not available at intermediate stations.

Upon demand by Railway Company's staff, Factory permit to be produced by passenger-holding this card travel ticket.

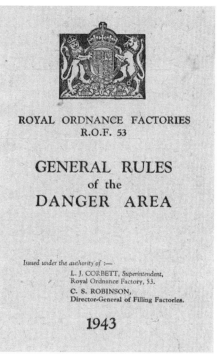

ROYAL ORDNANCE FACTORIES
R.O.F. 53

GENERAL RULES
of the
DANGER AREA

Issued under the authority of :—
L. J. CORBETT, Superintendent,
Royal Ordnance Factory, 53.
C. S. ROBINSON,
Director-General of Filling Factories.

1943

Passes and tickets (left) from Mrs Marshall's days at the Royal Ordnance factory at Pontypridd, together with the cover of the factory's Rules and Regulations (above)

sion. I sit and listen to some of the stories of those days and can now appreciate what some people did for the country at war.

My neighbour, Mrs Hannah Elizabeth Marshall, was born and bred in Pontypridd but she has lived for many years in Eardisley. Her husband, Cyril, who died in 1996, served with the King's Shropshire Light Infantry and the Durham Light Infantry in the war. During this time she worked as an ammunition inspector at Bridgend, travelling by bus and train. Mrs Marshall explained to me how the powder in the factory

Chief Inspector of Armaments Ammunition.

To Mrs Hannah Elizabeth Marshall on the occasion of your leaving the Department of the Chief Inspector of Armaments Ammunition. I wish to express my thanks to you for the essential service you have rendered the country whilst employed here from 26th August 1941 to 15th September 1945 and to extend to you the good wishes of the Department for your future well being

R E Smith

R.O.F., BRIDGEND.

INTERNAL BUS SERVICES

PRIORITY PASS

Name.... B. Marshall.... No.... 221.

could turn their skin and hair yellow if they were not covered up! Despite problems of all sorts, though, they seemed to have a wonderful spirit.

Mrs Marshall's leaving certificate (above left) from the Department of the Chief Inspector of Armaments Ammunition and (above right) her bus pass (the B is for Betty)

Chapter Three: The Two Garages

My father always enjoyed the bigger cars and I suppose they obviously made good taxis. I must admit that I enjoyed driving them as well when I got my licence to drive — especially the hefty Humber Super Snipe, with its spacious leather interior (and wonderful smell), column-change gear lever, its very long bonnet and wings, and its running boards. It was a novelty then just driving but driving these cars was a delight — especially as I was now driving them on the right side of the law and not constantly looking over my shoulder to see if someone was checking on me who knew I shouldn't be driving a car at all!

People in Eardisley will, I'm sure, also remember the Morris 16, the Hillman 16 and the Austin 18. These cars did service for years, from the mid-Forties — at least — right up till when my father finished in 1972. They all meant a lot to me and I feel affection for them. They all had the leather smell and the spacious interior, and I think they all had little fold-up tables for the back seats and pull-down blinds at the windows. The Morris and the Austin had temperature gauges situated outside but facing backwards, on the radiator filler cap, which meant that the driver had to have good eyesight.

Modello Garage was a lively and interesting place for me to grow up, with employees and customers coming and going all day. I remember a lot of people who worked there over the years. There was George Wearing, who lived at Dorstone and came to work on his Ariel 500 cc motorcycle, who had come to the garage after he left the navy. Then there was Walter Jenkins, who came to Modello as an apprentice. He had a girlfriend, Doris Evans, in Brilley he thought a lot of and one day, desperate to see her, he borrowed a friend's motorcycle (without permission) to drive to Brilley. In his haste he mistook a stone wall at Clyro for the road, had a nasty crash and was badly hurt. Eventually he was prosecuted and fined £5 (a lot in 1948) and not allowed to drive for twelve months. After he recovered he joined the REME as a regular. He became a sergeant, travelled to many parts of the world and now tells stories of his experiences, but he still has very happy and very detailed memories of his time working at Modello Garage — even remembering the registration numbers of some of the cars! Another person was Eric Clark, who lived in Woodseaves and used to ride his Sunbeam 350 cc motorcycle and sidecar down

One of R O Darling's blue buses outside Modello Works about 1941

to the garage and park it in the large shed at the back we called the bus shed (as that was where Darling's buses used to be kept). Sometimes when Eric had gone out on a job my pals and I used to take the Sunbeam out for a spin in the yard, bringing the sidecar up off the ground in a tight turn and riding the bike on two wheels with the sidecar up in the air — great fun! Eric was a grand chap. He had blond hair brushed straight back and well Brylcreemed; he spoke softly with a slight Welsh accent and occasionally gave us a lecture about riding his motorbike — but nothing to deter us from the next time!

A workman for R O Darling's in the 1930s, Robert Coudell (Bob), lived with his mother and father down a small track at the side of The Great Oak for many years. When he married he moved to Wales and there he eventually started a business selling commercial vehicles and buses. Now and again he still returns to Eardisley and then he reminisces about the old times. One evening, probably not long after the decimalization of British money in 1971, talking to Bob over a pint I happened to say I wish I had kept a One Pound note and Ten Shilling note for old times' sake. We talked a bit more about times gone by and then casually said we'd see one another again sometime and off we both went. When we next bumped into each other maybe twelve months later he gave me an envelope. Inside were a One Pound note and a Ten Shilling note. I still have them today.

Modello Garage ran the school car service from as far back as I can remember and in all the years the school car service was going there were no accidents. The local school children were brought to and from the Eardisley

Children in front of the Modello Garage Hillman school car in 1970. Left to right, back row, David Llewellyn, Colin Matthews, Jenny Llewellyn, William Llewellyn, Diane Lane (or possibly Debbie Raymond). Front row, David Goodwin, Tim Lane, Ann Goodwin (or possibly Lisa Merrick), David Bedford

school on a daily basis by the cars from the garage. There were three runs: Bollingham, Winforton and Kinnersley, morning and afternoon. Sometimes two cars would be involved and sometimes three. Kinnersley school was still going when my father started and at that time some of the children would be taken there, but at some stage Kinnersley school closed and then all the children came to Eardisley school. Sometimes, when my father was short of a regular driver for the school car, he would ask someone else to do the run, someone who he knew would be very capable of driving safely. It might be Mr Oliver Jones or it might be Mr Tom Stephens, a local farmer, again very experienced in driving. The main full-time driver was Mr Jim Williams, who started work with the Modello garage in 1951 and worked there until my father retired.

I am sure a lot of the children now grown-up have happy memories of those days and particularly of Jim Williams. He had volunteered as a regular soldier in 1946 and served with the engineers in East Africa. In 1951 he left the forces 'with' (as he put it) 'a suit, a bowler hat and a great coat — and the great coat I had to pay for'. (I learnt recently that his sister Stella had also done war service in the forces, serving in the WAAF [Women's Auxiliary Air Force] from October 1941 to April 1946, as Acting Corporal in the food-rationing stores at Madley. She left the forces on her birthday — 3 April — and for many years after that worked on the land.)

After Jim was demobbed he came to work as a mechanic and driver at Modello Works, and began driving the school cars. But he remained on the reserve list, that is (in his case), liable to be called up for the next five years. And in 1956 he was recalled — to go to Suez. He did not think much of it as he *was* just getting into the swing of civvy life and his five years on the reserve was almost up. But away he went. While Jim was away, Mr Tom Stephens and Mr Oliver Jones drove the school cars and were always willing to do so when required.

In January 1957 Jim's family were pleased to see him home again and he returned to his job at Modello Works. The children too were glad to have him back after his spell in Suez because they thought such a lot of him. He was very kind and generous with them, giving them sweets most days, but passing the sweet shop without stopping when there had been bad behaviour. He was soon putting lots of humour into the village again. Once he took a bet of £5 from another Eardisley chap that he wouldn't climb to the top of the very tall yew tree that used to be on the bridge in the middle of Eardisley. Jim had to take up a huge pair of ladies' underwear, which they had got from a basket of jumble, and hang it on the very highest branch. He managed to do this by using a broom handle to reach the last six foot. He was then offered another £5 to go up the tree again, and get the underwear back down, and again he won the bet without any trouble. Jim just thought what a good way this was to make £10!

Jim told me about a lady he and his sister, Stella Gale, used to visit, a Mrs Charles, who lived at Brook Cottage in Lower Welson. One day, finding her not at home, he decided to leave a message to say they had called, so he picked up an old slate, wrote a message on it, left it by the front door and went home. Arriving back home Mrs Charles found the slate and read the message 'Vicar called to see you today'. (Jim liked to say that the vicar never spoke to him after that, though I doubt if it's really true.)

After my father retired Jim and Stella took over the school contract in their own right. They bought an old black London taxi cab for the purpose, which was most unusual for Eardisley and great fun for the children to ride in. They used the swivel ashtrays to put their sweet papers in and when the taxi was not full they used the pull-down seats as desks and did their homework on them.

About the time Jim and Stella retired from the school cars they moved from Woonton, where they had lived for many years with their mother and Stella's husband, Stan, both of whom had now died. They moved to Weobley and there they did an enormous amount of fundraising for The Royal British Legion and for the charity that began life after the First World War as the British Limbless Ex-Servicemen's Association (BLESMA), and since 1993 has been called the Limbless Association. By 2004, when they finally finished this work, they had spent twenty years raising funds for the Limbless Association, and had collected more than £24,000.

My father and Ernie Crump ran a successful taxi service along with the garage business for forty years, taking people to weddings, funerals, hospitals

Jim Williams's retirement in July 1978. Left to right, back row, Susan Goodwin, Jane Brotherton, Jonathan Brotherton (or John Bedford), Mrs Angeline Preece (staff), Tony Raymond, Debbie Raymond, Susan (?) Jarrett, Mrs Stella Gale, unidentified child. Middle row, Mr Jim Williams, unidentified child, Mandy Smith, unidentified child. Front row, Hayley Bedford, Andrew Goodwin, unidentified child, Robert Raymond

and schools. In the days when the railways were still running the taxi service was always busy, as people would order a taxi to pick up them and their luggage and take them to or from the station. Most people in the village at some stage in their lives used the service and when I was old enough sometimes, if no other driver was available for a particular journey, I did it. So, over the years, as a family we got to know nearly everyone in the area to some extent.

The Modello taxi service was frequently called upon to take expectant mothers to hospital when the baby was on the way. Derek Smith remembers when my father took his wife, Beryl, to Hereford in July 1948. In the car were Derek and Beryl with Anne Davies (Mrs Walter Davies), the district nurse, as well as my father. As they approached The Portway my father looked back over his shoulder and cheerfully remarked 'This is where it usually happens!' Derek tells this little story laughing, remembering those times of Dad and his cars.

When I was very young, it was useful to have inside knowledge about when there was going to be a wedding because of a tradition involving the car taking the bride and groom away after the service. When we knew there was a wedding on, my pals and I wasted no time in getting a rope of some sort and making our way to the stile beside the 6-bar gate on glebe land on the other side of the road from Morgan's shop. Here we waited, sitting on the stile, a keen-eyed lookout watching the wedding car outside the lych-gate. Once the car with the bride and groom inside started to move off, the order was given for one of us to cross the road to the other side carrying one end of the rope. As the car drew near the rope would be lifted and made taut to make a barrier. At this point one of us would approach the bridegroom's window with hands cupped hoping to receive a generous handout. Sometimes we'd get a couple of shillings, but if we were lucky we might get a ten bob note. Once we'd got the money we would drop the rope to the delight of the happy couple and the car was able to go on its way — sometimes only to find another rope by the Doctor's bridge!

Mr Oliver Jones, the father of one of my best pals, Brian (usually known as Nowt), had the second garage in Eardisley, just round the corner from The Strand, on the Almeley road. Mr Jones was a very good engineer. He must also have had a lot of patience as groups of us would hang around the garage, doing something or other that seemed important to us — something like mending punctures in our bikes — and I am sure we must have been in his way. Sometimes we would be up in the loft above the workshop floor when he was doing some delicate operation on a vehicle and not far away other members of staff might be doing something else. Suddenly, from high above, one of us lads would do a Tarzan act, swinging through the jungle on a rope, narrowly missing Mr Jones, the other men and the vehicles, and barely avoiding injury to ourselves. Full of the excitement of the game, we would not realize just how far down the rope we were holding it — once we'd taken off from the loft there would be no second chance to grab the rope further up.

Mr Oliver Jones, Nowt's father, in the 1940s or '50s

And then there was the telephone — an old-fashioned machine even then that hung on the wall. You held the earpiece in one hand and spoke into a separate piece you held in the other hand. I don't think that we actually made calls with the telephone, but we certainly had fun pretending to do so and probably imitating grown-ups' telephone conversations we'd heard.

Today I still wonder at Mr Jones putting up with the trouble we must have given him as lads. If we were not causing havoc in any other way we were probably out firing up the old traction engine in the yard — with cardboard and sticks or anything we could lay our hands on. The traction engine, which was mainly stationary in the yard, was great fun for us, and in a way Mr Jones encouraged us to learn about the way it operated, as long as we were careful. Sometimes though, as the smell of the steam rose into the air and the large flywheel on the side of the engine began to turn as we opened up the steam valve, things got close to being dangerous, and she moved a few yards. Maybe it's as well we could not get any coal. Otherwise we might just have given her a road test — which might not have pleased our local bobby.

When he was seven or eight, Nowt had gone with his father to collect this steam engine, and sixty-odd years later he recalls the whole story in great detail. 'All men', he says, 'are boys at heart'.

'All men are boys at heart': the steam engine
— as recalled by Brian (Nowt) Jones

During the time my lifelong friend has been researching this book, we have discussed the old traction engine on which as children and teenagers of the late Forties and early Fifties we used to play and experiment with steam-raising. Eventually the question was asked 'Where did it come from and to where did it go?' This short narrative will recall to the best of my fallible memory the day the traction engine came to the garage.

It is necessary to set the scene for this, my father's last indulgence. Although a true motor engineer, my father had a lifelong respect and passion for 'steam'. This may have come about from boyhood days, in the family wheelwright business and later on the farm, when, for a child, the most exciting event would be the arrival of the travelling 'tack' — either to saw in the former enterprise, or to thresh in the latter. There again, it may have been that in his apprenticeship days before the Great War he would have had contact with the superior steam cars of those early days — superior, that is, in performance and reliability. This abiding interest in steam was kept alive by the occasional repair of, and spare part manufacture for, the various steam engines that were not uncommon until electrification at about the time of the Second World War. Many of these engines and tractions were used in the timber trade, but just after the war this was rapidly re-equipping with ex-War Department vehicles, leaving the portable engines and tractions redundant, mostly to be cut up for scrap metal.

The talk in workshops and pubs, therefore, was very often talk of change and redundant machinery. Father was, of course, very tempted to join in the general euphoria of post-war years by spending some of his hard-earned money (as well as some that, though hard-earned, had not been received). Many hours during the war had been spent keeping the local road-transport company vehicles on the road and one of these had been largely committed to the collection and distribution of timber from around our district. So it was that from the sawyers and fellers Father got to hear about a traction engine which had spent the war years powering an on-site sawmill on the north side of Merbach Hill, directly opposite Eardisley across the river Wye.

Plans were set afoot: part of the outstanding repair cost would be set against the hire of the necessary equipment and gang of men to extract and deliver the traction to Eardisley — no mean task since the traction weighed about ten tons and required removal from a site high in the woods. The gang, as I recall, consisted of two drivers and a number of labourers. The late Bill Bounds, recently returned from military service, drove a standard Fordson winch tractor (ballast weights front and timber winch rear), and the late Arthur Barnett a short-wheelbase Bedford tipper-truck ballasted with three tons of stone. Several timber men, including the late Frank Preece, were there to act as chockers and ropemen. (While the extraction exercise was going on, incidentally, Frank took me aside to show me the only stream in the world that runs uphill.)

Father, of course, took pride of place as steersman of his new toy.

Apart from the 'stream!!' I can remember little about the extraction of the engine and our descent down the hill, but suffice it to say that by the time we arrived at Eddie Price's — Weston Farm — everyone was very thirsty. So a cider stop was made. Eddie being a good customer of Father's, his appreciation took liquid form, with the result that the entourage set forth for home from Weston Farm in a very jolly state, the tractor pulling the traction and the Bedford acting as a brake van behind. The whole lot, coupled-up together, moved along in a dignified — if zigzag — way, as Father overcompensated the line of direction with very slack steering while winding on the wooden brake block — not helped, of course, by the now oblivious infant (my baby brother) who had gone to sleep on his shoulder.

They crossed Bredwardine bridge and successfully negotiated the treacherous Letton road. (The timber on the river bank had been felled, and so there was nothing to camouflage the sheer drop to the river, which for years frightened this young traveller passing that way.) The relief everyone felt at reaching Letton necessitated a short stop at The Swan — to allow the tractor to cool off and the crew to steady their nerves before tackling the infamous Letton Lane. Then it was off again. By now, of course, things were moving at a fine pace and so a quick stop at Crow Farm — to celebrate the safe passage with Jim Price — seemed appropriate.

I had been riding with Arthur in the brake lorry and must have gone to sleep because the next memory I have is of a lot of action on the gradient of the south side of Eardisley rail bridge, where, due to a missed gear, the winch rope had to be used to get moving. In stately fashion the entourage passed through the village until the New Inn corner, but after several shunts this was

'The relief everyone felt at reaching Letton necessitated a short stop at The Swan.'

negotiated and the traction was finally delivered to its new home. For me it was straight to bed, but for the grown-ups the celebrations continued long into the night at The New Inn.

Brian has told you of the escapades that the traction afforded a whole generation of village children. The stress on Mum was something else. For starters there was a blocked view from her sitting-room window. Then there were the endless sooty, oily, filthy rags to wash, not to mention occasional sooty specks getting onto the pristine washing on her clothes-line from our illicit firings of the engine. So there was some flak about at home. But Father was adamant that this self-indulgence was worthwhile — as a steam cleaner! To use a modern expression, 'In your dreams, Dad!' The steam cleaning of course never happened, but we did have *hours* of pleasure with the traction and even this, I am sure, was as nothing compared to Dad's joy in at last owning a traction engine.

What happened to it? Well, that's quite strange. After I took out indentures with Father, on the odd occasion he would have me recast the fire plug and seal off the corroded boiler tubes so that we could burn the workshop waste and watch the flywheel and gears go round. Eventually National Service beckoned and I joined with alacrity — not realizing the position I had left my father in. In 1956 he had severe bronchitis, which took a lot of getting over. His brother Bernard (Uncle Bern), who was at that time doing the bookwork, kept the business going but it was a close-run thing, necessitating the selling of much of the accumulated scrap, including the — by now famous — traction.

It's funny how easily things are forgotten. During my research for the Eardisley History Group, Roy Thomas told me that the traction engine left Eardisley, as it had arrived, being towed through the village to the station. There it was loaded onto a flat car, never to be seen again.

It was a good place for us at Mr Jones's garage as nobody seemed to bother us, so we all congregated there. Later we went from pushbikes to motorcycles, and regularly had spanners, spark plugs and timing chains all over the place. Most of us had been able to ride from an early age — as young as six or seven — as the bigger boys would teach the little ones. I remember being so small when I learnt to ride that for the first few times the bigger boys — my brother, Ken Townsend and John Jones from The Derry — had to put up bales of straw in the fields. They would have to run with me and the bike to start us off round the field as my legs wouldn't reach the ground. Then, as the motorcycle was so big, the only way to get me off was for the bigger boys to catch me on the way round or put bales of straw so that I could come in to land on them. I think they thought I was a Japanese kamikaze: happy to face certain death!

There was always a favourite car parked at the garage, and when the coast was clear it would be a good time to give it a test run. I started doing this at quite a young age. A long time later Mrs Anne Davies (wife of Mr Walter Davies), who when I was young lived in the Bank House, told me this little story. 'Some years back I was walking down the village past Modello garage. I saw this car coming down the yard, around the fuel pumps by the side of the main road, and back up into the bus shed — and there appeared to be noone driving it. But after I walked up the yard I saw you getting out of the car, all three foot six of you!' Astonishingly she just smiled and went on her way. A close encounter!

I was quite a good driver by the age of about nine years. At least I thought

Mrs Rose Jones, wife of Mr Oliver Jones and mother of my friend Nowt. Mrs Jones was warm, friendly and easy-going, and had a large happy family. (Very often she had half the village children under her roof as well.) She put up with a lot without getting cross or bothered.
I have a feeling that she was interested in everything that was going on and liked to keep in touch.

so, if nobody else did, and I had plenty of experience by then. Sometimes I would let one or two of my pals have a drive but some of them hadn't driven much, so I would have to show them what the controls did … after a few leaps and bounds they would get the idea.

On one occasion, while I was having a little drive round the yard, one of my pals, Roy, asked me if he could have a go at driving. He had never driven before so I had to show him how to drive, and, as we were at the bottom end of the bus shed, Roy would have to go backwards out of the shed (where there were other cars parked).

After a quick verbal lesson of about thirty seconds, Roy was ready for a drive. Roy, myself and the Vauxhall, with its strong towing bar and hitch on the back, shot backwards at a very fast speed. There was a loud crash as we shot straight

Fixing a broken wheel, 1950s. Left to right, David Knights, Desmond Jarrett, Robert Knights, me, [just visible behind] Popper (Nowt's younger brother, Trevor), Roy Thomas, Nick. (Nowt probably took the photo.) This Austin 10 van was used by Mr Brierley for his meat deliveries after he gave up using a pony and trap, but by the time of this picture it belonged to Nowt's father, who used it (when we were not borrowing it for jaunts) as a garage breakdown vehicle. We used to take it out quite often on a Sunday afternoon, taking it in turns to drive. The roof was a bit loose and it lifted up in the wind if we drove too fast, so someone would have to hold on to it to stop it taking off. Before this picture was taken, I had been driving. I remember we had been going along the road from Builth to Glasbury; the others were urging me to go faster and faster but I had a feeling that there was a wobble in one of the back wheels. Eventually we stopped to check and then we found that the wheel was literally disintegrating and the spokes were coming loose. We changed the wheel at the roadside and then cautiously drove on to Hay and to H V Webb's, where I was working at the time. Of course the place was closed as it was Sunday afternoon, but I managed to break in and find the kit to pump up the spare wheel.

into the front of a beautiful new Singer tourer sports car. Duck-egg blue in colour, the metal on the Singer was strong, but not as strong as the towing hitch on the Vauxhall.

Roy ran for home but I was already home so I couldn't run far. I then thought the best thing I could do was try and repair the damage. After spending five or ten minutes trying to straighten out the bent bits, I decided the car could do with a polish. I mixed some car polish up with a drop or two of paraffin and rubbed the mixture all over the front of the car. Maybe the damaged look would go away. It didn't.

Next day, after a day working at Kitty Darling's — and I should say a very worrying day, I arrived home. My father called me over to him and I tried to talk my way out it. Then he delivered the required punishment — but much less than I deserved. He really did seem to be sorry that he had to punish me and to be very restrained and reasonable. He did not go off the deep end — as the fathers of many children I knew would have done. I always admired Dad for that. It wasn't the only time he had to pick up the pieces for me. Many times in later years he came to rescue me when I'd ditched a car or my motorbike had broken down. I hope he felt I gave him something back in return for the problems I caused him.

The van Nowt's father used as a breakdown vehicle had previously belonged to Mr Brierley the butcher, who used it for meat deliveries after the horse-and-cart days — quite a change from meat to tools. When we were old enough to drive cars Mr Jones often used to let us borrow this van to go out on jaunts of one sort or another, taking turns to drive.

Nowt was telling me recently about a time when his father was preparing a customer's vehicle for some sort of inspection. (I think it was an early version of the MOT test.) This vehicle had been in a bad state of repair and so Mr Jones had done a lot of work on it before notifying the inspector that he was ready, but eventually the inspector came out from Hereford, checked the vehicle over and passed it as all right. Afterwards, glancing round and making his way towards the breakdown van, the inspector suggested they had better have a look at the other vehicles while he was there. His inspection did not take long and without much hesitation he said to Nowt's father, 'Mr Jones, you must take this van off the road immediately as it has had its day and is probably dangerous'. This was sad news for Mr Jones but even sadder for us lads as we remembered all the happy times we had had driving round in her. But maybe it was for the best. We had already had a few close shaves: apart from the time when the rear wheel disintegrated, we had almost lost the roof many times — the fact that we didn't was due to the skills of the person sitting on the floor in the back holding it in place (while others were trying to sit comfortably on the floor among the spanners, the toolbox and the spare half gallon of fuel). At least we still had the wonderful memories.

Chapter Four: Motorcycles

Once, walking back from the station with Nowt — we were about eight at the time — as we passed Mr Wilfred Morgan's shop next to the telephone exchange, we saw a motorcycle parked at the back of the shop. I knew the owner, Tom Hicks, who I expect had left it there while he went off shopping, and thought he wouldn't mind if I had a little spin round the field where it was parked. Tom's brother-in-law, Cyril Morgan, saw me wondering whether I should have a ride and was all for it. So I kicked the bike up and off I went. It went very well, considering it was on grass. 'Come on, Knifer!', Cyril kept shouting (using his nickname for me, which never really caught on with anyone else). Whenever I opened the throttle the back wheel skidded from side to side — especially if I had just hit a cow pat — which Cyril egged me on to do enthusiastically! In the middle of all this, Tom came back and caught me on his bike, it and me covered in cow pat. Not surprisingly he wasn't too pleased — but, the character he was, he didn't *really* mind — people then seemed very tolerant.

The first motorcycle that my mates and I actually bought — when we were about eleven — we acquired for £5 from Mr Dennis Jones, who lived at Willersley. (Dennis was the brother of Vic Jones, who is still often to be seen sitting on the bench outside the lych-gate). The bike, which Mr Jones had laid up under some bales of straw with galvanized sheeting as a roof, was a 250 cc Rudge but it was fitted with an OHV (overhead valve) Jap engine. I remember the times we spent trying to get the engine to run properly, as the magneto, which is the part that creates the spark, was very poor. I think we spent as much time repairing as we did riding but eventually we got it going quite well. After that mostly we had some motorcycle or other, which we had acquired for a couple of pounds or as a swap. Fuel was a slight problem but Nowt's father's and my father's garages both had fuel pumps and occasionally the pumps would 'leak' a pint or two. The 'leaked' fuel, mixed with a drop of TVO, enabled us to get a few rides in.

When we had had our first motorcycle a while we got to hear of a chap over by Titley who wanted a Rudge motorcycle. So we made contact with him and did a deal to exchange the Rudge for a 1926 350 cc Sunbeam — an old bike but very interesting, with its beaded-edge wheels and square fuel tank. Although the Sunbeam was not running we were confident it would not take us long to get it going, but in the meantime it had to be brought back from somewhere Titley way to Eardisley. As I had drawn the short straw I was the one who had to go and fetch it. (I would have been about twelve years old at this time.)

Somehow I managed to get myself over to Titley and to the gentleman we were doing the deal with. I don't remember much about him except that he seemed very tall, and had a beard — I was more interested in getting the bike back to Jones's garage to prepare it for us to use. As the engine would not start and we had no trailer the only choice was to tow the bike. So, as it was a quiet Sunday afternoon and there wasn't much traffic about then anyhow, that's what we did. The gentleman, who owned an Austin 7 open tourer, reversed it up the yard and tied a towrope between the car and the Sunbeam. As I got on the bike

to be towed back to Eardisley, I remember thinking rather apprehensively that it was a fair distance to be towed behind a car and hoping he wouldn't break the sound barrier. I was right to be nervous because I soon found out that the brakes of the Sunbeam were pretty well non-existent. We drove to Eardisley along the little byroads, which meant quite a lot of corners and hills. It was not long before I was having to improvise with the brakes, as one minute the towrope was tight and the next minute the front wheel of the bike was running over it. I was able to overcome this dangerous tendency by putting the bike in low gear and braking with the clutch as required. It was one time when I was grateful the engine wouldn't start. Arriving back at Nowt's garage, I was *very* relieved to park the Sunbeam up! My mates and I then spent the rest of the afternoon discussing the important question of what we were going to do to get it running and in good condition.

Oliver Jones with his daughter Marjorie and two sons, Bill and Brian, in Spring 1938. Bill is standing to the right of the pram and Brian — my friend Nowt — is in the pram. Nowt says the four of them would just have returned from a walk 'up the Drails' (the area now called The Field). At this time of year the Drails would have been a mass of daffodils — as we can imagine from the bunches of flowers held by Mr Jones and Marjorie in the picture.

We worked on it for a week or so, carrying out repairs and replacing oils, but eventually it was ready to be taken for a run, and the following Sunday afternoon we prepared to take it down through the village to the Park road behind Eardisley church, which was a private road. I won the toss to decide who would be having the pleasure of driving. So, after checking that we had got enough fuel, I mounted the bike, followed very quickly by Nowt and Frank. Roy Thomas stood at the T-junction by The New Inn, watching for traffic coming down the village — usually there wasn't much in those days and being a Sunday it was very quiet. After Roy had given us the all clear, the three of us took off down the road, followed by a cloud of white smoke. There was a lot of misfiring of the engine as we turned the corner for the bottom of the village, and having Nowt and Frank behind me didn't leave me much room to control the bike, but we were on our way.

We got as far as Mr Wynne's shop (where Janet's newsagent's used to be) when the one and only car about that day arrived from the Kington road. It was The Law in the shape of Sergeant Gregg — with his wife, and off duty, but for some reason in his uniform. We came to a halt of course and Sergeant Gregg booked us. Glumly we pushed the bike to Modello Garage (which was nearer than where we'd come from) and we all spent the rest of the day across the fields rehearsing what we would say in court. I think the law had already done its job, though. We never heard any more about it. We survived to ride again but only on private property or in fields and of course we were able to go on the roads when we were old enough to get a licence.

Derry Barker, behind, and Nowt on the Sunbeam on the old Eardisley to Almeley railway line — early Fifties. I am not sure who the young boy in the background is.

Some time later, when Nowt had just modified the brakes on the Sunbeam, we decided to test them on the old Eardisley to Almeley railway line. The line hadn't been used for some time and the rails had been taken up, so it made a good track for us to ride the motorcycles, which we did on many occasions. At this time we were garaging the bike in one of the platelayers' huts made out of railway sleepers at the side of the line, so we took it out of its hiding place and the three of us (me, Nowt and Roy) set off. We push-started it and it took off down the railway track, with me on the front and the other two sat behind me. Eventually we got the bike in top gear and, as we were enjoying ourselves sailing along at a good speed, I left it till the last minute to test the brakes. Suddenly I saw a barbed wire fence stretching right across the line only a few yards ahead. I applied the brakes as instructed and nothing happened. At least, the only thing that did happen was that I found myself

Me, on the BSA Bantam I used for scrambling, outside Modello Works, with Brook House in the background — about 1953

Another picture, taken at about the same time, of me on the BSA Bantam

alone on the bike — Nowt and Roy had hastily jumped ship. As I didn't really want to go through the barbed wire fence, I could only take a short cut over the railway embankment — which I did, bike and all. The consequences were not as serious as they might have been: my overalls went for a Burton (which I wouldn't have minded but they were new) and the barbed wire fence cut my right arm as I descended down the side of the embankment. I still have the scar to prove it. The funny thing is, I had been to the dentist in Hay that morning — Foster and Fairey, or something like that, I think they were called. I had had gas and while I was under had a nightmarish dream — all a bit vague really — about drastic events on the motorcycle. Was it a premonition? Well, maybe, but I did have motorbikes on my mind nearly all the time in those days! Anyhow, we didn't try a ride like that again without first making sure the brakes worked.

Riding motorcycles to us then as lads was great fun. It was exciting to be able to work and earn enough money to buy an old motorcycle very cheaply and find private ground to ride on. Looking back on those days I feel the people — especially some of the farmers — must have been very good and tolerant as they never appeared to mind us riding on their land, sometimes without permission (which I now appreciate).

When we got to sixteen and were at last old enough to have motorcycle licences, we each began to want to have our own motorcycle. One of the first to have his own bike was someone a little older than me, Keith Needes. Keith lived in The Malt House in Winforton, next to Winforton Hall, but by the time we were into our 'legal' motorcycle days he had become one of us and spent most of his time in Eardisley. Keith rode a 250 cc OHV C11 BSA and one Monday evening he set off from Winforton to come to the pictures at Eardisley village hall, as he often did. On the Eardisley side of the cottages on the Winforton main road was a Hillman car which had broken down with a split water hose. The car was at the side of the road and the driver, Mr David Powell (Eardisley's current David Powell), who at that time was living at Welshwood, was checking the problem. He heard a motorcycle coming but took no notice as that was quite normal. But suddenly there was a terrific crash and David and the car were bumped several yards down the road. Keith appeared not to have seen the car and to have driven into the rear of it, with his motorcycle running up and over the car and landing on the road beyond. With crash helmets rarely being worn in those days, Keith was badly hurt and regained consciousness only after a week in hospital. Everyone was very relieved — I remember calling at his home every day on my way home from work, hoping for good news of him. Thankfully, David was not hurt.

Eventually things turned out all right and Keith got better to ride again. The 250 BSA was badly damaged but it was a nice bike and so I bought it from Keith and repaired it. I rode it for some time before selling it on to a Mr John Powell, who at that time was in the RAF and used the bike for going to and from his camp. I don't know what happened to the bike after that.

Most of us who had motorcycles then had crashes one way or another. Derry Barker crashed his lovely 350 cc BSA at the bottom of Eardisley village by Wharf corner. Derry was riding towards the village when suddenly he was confronted by an A40 van driven by Mr Bill Nicholas. At that time Mr Nicholas lived at The Wharf and had called in there for his lunch. While he was turning the van out and back onto the road to return to Hereford,

Derry Barker receiving moral support from Joy (left in picture) and Brynis Lloyd after badly damaging his leg and foot in a motorcycling accident at Wharf corner — mid-Fifties

Keith Needes on Derry Barker's motorcycle on the Kington road — early Fifties

Derry crashed into it and was badly hurt. He recovered from the accident but I think even now, fifty years later, he still has problems with the leg and foot that were injured.

One of my accidents was with another BSA. This was a 250 cc that I had reconditioned and sprayed what I thought was a lovely silvery blue. (I thought a lot of my motorcycles — I think we all did.) One Saturday lunchtime I was returning from my work at H V Webb's in Hay-on-Wye across the Woodseaves back road to Eardisley, hurrying to meet the lads to go swimming. (I was driving quite fast, though when I was interviewed by PC Barker later my estimate of my speed dropped a little!). I got as far as the sharp bend on the Eardisley side of Mr Whittall's farm, where the hedges and banks are quite high so that you can't see what is coming. Suddenly, from out of nowhere, a large yellow van appeared, taking up most of the roadway on the bend. It all happened very quickly. There was nowhere for me to go, no choice but to steer through the gap — about a foot wide — between the bank and the van. I got through the gap but without my motorcycle (and right boot) and went flying through the air, landing in the middle of the road about ten yards behind the van, facing the way I had just come from.

With no crash helmet I was very lucky to escape serious injury or even death. But, apart from my pride being hurt, my only injury was some damage to my right leg. I needed a few weeks in bed to recover and had to put up with a visit from the law, but before long I was all right to enjoy riding motorcycles again. I repaired my BSA and later sold it to Mr Arthur Barnet, who lived in Kinnersley and worked for the county council. He rode the bike for many years afterwards.

Many people in Eardisley will remember Cecil Amos — again one of the lads who lived in Winforton but spent a lot of his time in Eardisley. He was the leader of the pack as far as motorcycles were concerned, as he always had the best machine of us all, usually a brand new one. When he rode up to us on a 350 cc Matchless, with dual seat and sprung-frame suspension, and put it through its paces, we all looked at it longingly. Cecil never appeared to hurt himself apart from a few bumps now and again, although his speeds, especially through Eardisley, were excessive. He seemed not to touch the road as he went over the Doctor's bridge before screeching on towards Kington, the footrest scraping the tarmac as he leaned over at speed at Bollingham on the sharp bends.

I remember on one occasion Cecil had changed his Matchless for a brand new AJS 600 cc Twin, which was the envy of us all. So when he said to me, 'Jump on the back of this lovely machine' I did so without hesitation, eagerly looking forward to a trip to Kington and back. Again, we had no helmets or other protective clothing in those days. Looking back, it was ridiculous, but at the time no-one seemed to think of the danger — just ride and enjoy it.

Taking off from Tram Square, where we usually met up before going off for trips, Cecil, with me on the back, headed off for Kington and we enjoyed the trip at quite high speed. I was hoping Cecil would let me ride the bike back myself, with him on the back seat, but he did not mention that. So we headed back to Eardisley as before, again at high speed (or so it seemed), the wind blowing through our hair and our shirts.

When we came to the top of Bollingham, from where it is downhill most of the way to the village, Cecil turned to me and, shouting to make himself heard above the noise of the wind, said, 'Lean forward. We will test her down here'. He leaned forward. So did I — there was no option as the wind generated by our speed was so strong. Going downhill he opened the throttle to full and we reached what must have been a terrifically high speed — I could not see the speedometer from my position but it must have been the AJS's maximum speed.

There are some horrible blind spots on the road down from Bollingham, where the road goes up and down. Just as we reached maximum speed we saw in one of those blind spots, not far off, a herd of cattle being driven up the hill by a farmer with his dog. It was a blessing that Cecil was a skilled driver. There was *just* enough time for him to put on the brakes, change down through the gearbox very rapidly and bring the bike to a halt (with him sitting almost on the handlebars and me where he should have been). What a relief! I never rode on the back with Cecil again.

I did ride on a bike Cecil had helped to build. He and another friend, Kenneth Hammond, built a scramble bike out of a 250 cc Ariel, but Cecil would never himself ride at scrambles: I never knew why, as he was an excellent rider on the roads — apart from his speeds! The Ariel was a great bike and they had made a good job of it. As Cecil did not want to ride it I asked him if I could. Without hesitation he said, 'Of course you can'. I was very pleased and rode the Ariel at several meetings. If the race was one where you had to kick-start the bike when the flag went down to start the race, I usually got away to a very good start, as one kick and I'd be away. But it was not very long before I could hear the roar of the other bikes, tight on my heels, overtaking me and leaving me covered in mud. I did not mind too much as I just enjoyed the races. I entered as many as I could and ended up tired and soaked in mud. The smell of Castrol R and the general atmosphere at those events linger in my memory ... wonderful days.

As time went on we got old enough to have driving licences and move on to other things. Those early days of our motorcycles taught us a lot about engines and how to repair and improvise — I think that learning has been very important to me and my pals and has helped us with our lives as we have grown older.

Sports and carnivals have been held in Eardisley for many years, with people from the village and much of the surrounding areas taking part. Some years ago even horseracing and occasional grass-tracking were held in the field at the back of the village hall. At one such grass-track meeting, the track was roped off to keep the spectators out. The track consisted of the ropes going round in a circle with a square piece of roped area for the riders and bikes to enter. The evening before the race was held a few of the local lads decided to have a ride round the track on their own motorcycles. Everyone was having great fun until Ken Townsend began to ride round the *outside* of the ropes. Ken had forgotten about the ropes marking the entry and exit points which stuck out at right angles to the rest of the ropes. When he came up against the rope crossing his path he came to a sudden halt, but his motorcycle carried on. After picking himself and his bike up he dusted himself off and started all over again.

Ladies' football team at the Eardisley carnival in the 1970s.
Left to right, back row, Ev Hatcher, unidentified lady holding rattle,
Elizabeth Wood, Ann Wood, Elsie Taylor, May Willford, Norah Nicholas.
Front, Doreen Payne, Josephine Burgoyne, Shirley Allan (my sister), Pat Townsend,
Mabel Townsend

Chapter Five: Pals

My two best pals were Elwyn Nicholas (Nick) and Brian Jones (Nowt). Elwyn Nicholas, who lived at The Wharf at the bottom of Eardisley, became one of my best mates from a very early time in our lives and we grew up together having many good times and adventures. He lived with his mother and father, William (Bill) and Florence Nicholas, and his brother, John. As far as I know the family had lived in Eardisley for a long time and I think Bill worked in the grocery trade. Elwyn's mother and father always made me welcome in their home and I spent a lot of time down there. They treated me as though I was one of the family and later on in life Mrs Nicholas even used to say to people, 'This is our adopted son'. I feel I really did have that kind of a bond with them. Bill died at the young age of 60 and was greatly missed by many people. He had done a lot for the church and the community, serving as an officer in the Fire Brigade, and, like Elwyn, he loved to have a joke, especially about the funny things that had happened when they were called out to a fire.

Nick was tidier than Nowt (tidier than me too). (His dad always wore a bow tie and, as I remember him, was very smart.) Nick was more conservative and keener to get on with things than Nowt; he had a little bit of 'front'. He had a keen eye — he was one of the best shots of all of us, with a catapult and with a bow and arrow, and leaned towards ball games, especially football. He enjoyed riding his bicycle and used to set the seat very high, saying it stretched his legs. (I think it may well have done this as he turned out to be the tallest of us.) He had a good nature and was always smiling and joking about things. Sleeping out in the copse, as we did on several occasions, he would tell stories enthusiastically, making them all, from cowboy yarns to ghost tales, sound very real. One of his favourite tricks was the dead-man's-finger joke. This was a gruesome bit of nonsense involving a small box with a hole in the bottom and some bloody-looking bandages (probably soaked in food-colouring or paint). Elwyn would push one of his fingers through the hole and wrap the 'bloody' bandage round the base of his finger, concealing the hole in the box. Then he would use his other hand to lift the lid of the box so that gullible people who did not know the trick could be shown the horrible contents of his box — 'a dead man's finger'!

Outside Ashcroft, left to right, me, holding a banjo, Nowt and Nick, about 1948. Just after this photo was taken, I gave the banjo to Trevor Lewis, who lived at Cookshell in Almeley with a Mr and Mrs Price. (I knew him because, like me, he sometimes did work for Kitty Darling.) I swapped my banjo for Trevor's black leather jacket — he was quite a lot older than me, probably about 18 in 1948, but I remember him as a slight person and so the jacket fitted me all right.

Nowt was the smallest of us: that was why he came to be called Nowt. Sometimes we used to go together to The Firs, which is next door to the Methodist chapel, to see another pal, Gordon Holmes, who lived there, and when Gordon's Auntie Eileen saw Brian she used to say 'There's nowt of him!' (Actually, when we grew up Nowt was one of the bigger chaps.) He was adventurous and what we'd now call laid-back — he had the attitude that there's always tomorrow. He was very mechanically minded and was always improvising things. When he was in short trousers I remember him with a fringe of blackish hair, a little unruly sometimes, wearing an open-necked shirt and with his socks falling down round his ankles. He and I have seen and done many things together over the years, (*some* of which I can write about!) and we are still pals today. His father, Oliver Jones, owned one of the garages in the village and this was the source of a lot of the wonderful times we had as boys.

On one occasion Nowt and I took a trip to Hay-on-Wye. It was quite an adventure for us — we must have been all of eight or nine. As the train pulled out of Eardisley station we settled down, just the two of us, to light up one of our Woodbines which we had from an open-top five-Woodbine packet. It didn't last long as most of the cigarette was soggy wet from our mouths — I think we would have been better off eating it. Arriving at Hay we stepped off the train and headed for town. We spent some time looking around and then came upon a shop selling chocolate 'off coupons'. We were very surprised to see you did not need coupons and decided to buy a bar each. We enjoyed eating the chocolate but by the time we arrived back in Eardisley we had discovered the reason why you didn't need coupons — it should have been obvious from where we had bought it — Mr Nutt's, the chemist's — and from its name — Ex Lax!

Sometimes on a weekend my pals and I would go across to the fields next to the old railway line from Eardisley to Almeley, where there was a donkey, and challenge one another who could ride on him for the longest — which usually was in seconds rather than minutes.

One day Nowt decided that if two of us got on the donkey he wouldn't be able to throw us off so quickly. So we caught the donkey and both of us got on him, which he didn't take too kindly to and he took off with us both on his back. Down the embankment he charged and then he promptly put his head down to the ground. At the same time up came his rear end, sending us flying through the air like a pair of trapeze artists. As I was on the front of the donkey, I hit the ground first, followed very promptly by Nowt, who landed directly on top of me. Needless to say, it took the wind out of my sails. After a while, thinking about this new trick the three of us had learned, I thought it might be a good idea if Nowt sat at the front of the donkey and I at the back. We tried this with the same result as before except that this time Nowt discovered how I had felt the first time and didn't laugh so much!

Four of my pals in about 1952. Left to right, Popper (Trevor Jones), Roy Thomas, Nowt and Nick

Sometimes riding the donkey got a little dangerous when he really got annoyed. On one occasion, I remember Humphrey Plumstead seemed to be going well until the donkey decided to go off up the railway embankment at quite an angle. As the donkey's back was very slippery Humphrey slid off the rear and landed directly behind the donkey's hindquarters, allowing him to kick out with both legs. My own and Nowt's fall seemed nothing to the severe bump Humphrey received but he got over it to ride again another day.

When I was young I was quite inventive. When I was about eight I acquired — from my cousin, I think — a few pieces of 1" film, each a few yards long, of Mickey Mouse. Perhaps my cousin gave me the film because he had no means of operating it but I remember somehow managing to see some jerky animated sequences — Mickey launching a ship and picking apples — by doing something with a wind-up gramophone. Later, when I was about fifteen, I decided to make a motorized lawn-mower and eventually succeeded by combining a push mower with a motorized invalid chair.

I can't remember how old we were when we got into photography. What I do remember is a few of us using Nowt's sitting room with the curtains drawn as a dark-room. We were busy with exposed film and a tank of developing fluid (I can't remember what we used as a container) and Nowt's Auntie Ethel was

*Three men in a boat on the river Wye —
mid-Fifties. In front, me and Derry Barker,
behind, Graham Jones*

banging on the door to come in. I don't really know why she was banging on the door or why we didn't want her in but I remember that we ended up climbing out of the window to escape.

Another time, again at Nowt's, we were playing with part of a model aeroplane of mine. We had just the engine of this, about fist-sized — a real working diesel engine, about $1/8$ hp — with a propeller attached, clamped in a vice on the kitchen table. We fired up the engine and the propeller soon began to spin so fast that you couldn't see it any more. I decided to open up the throttle a bit more and put my hand in to make the adjustment. The propeller, though invisible, was very definitely there — and moving with huge force, because it caught my thumb very painfully and I still have a dent to prove it.

Later I was often glued to the wireless. I'd get as close as I could to the set to listen to *The Navy Lark, Round the Horn, The Goons, ITMA* and *Have a Go* with Wilfred Pickles and Mabel — 'Give him the money, Mabel' used to be his catch-phrase. Then there was *Just William* and various thrillers, *The Madison Case*, Valentine Dyall as The Man in Black in *Appointment with Fear* and, best of all, Dick Barton. Nick, Nowt and I all followed the adventures of Dick and his friends Snowy White and Jock Anderson, and we often imagined ourselves helping them out of some predicament or other.

The three of us, Nowt, Nick and I, were very close. We always went about together but we had other pals, such as Desmond Jarrett (who lived with his grandparents, Eardisley's village policeman and his wife) and Graham Jones (son of Sidney Jones the coal merchant, who was the business partner of Mr Walter Howells). Then there was Frank Moulton (Norah Nicholas's brother), always the most daring of us, diving down into salmon holes in the river amongst the metal and concrete debris to see how long he could stay under the water, and Roy Thomas, son of May Thomas (who had earlier run the laundry) and grandson of Mr and Mrs Roly Webb at the Institute. Clive Davies from Castle Farm, where we often played cricket on the front lawn, was one of the lads and sometimes his sisters, Olive (now Olive Morgan), Myra and Jill, joined in as well. Derry and Ron Barker (sons of a later village policeman) were usually around. Derry was steady and quiet, soft-spoken, always clean, tidy and presentable — I don't remember him doing the adventurous things much, like swimming in the Sheep Dip Brook at Parsonage Farm with us, but we all liked him. Ron was more daring than his brother: he had a cheeky smile. If he wasn't throwing a ball up into the gutter on the roof of the school (so that he had to climb up and recover it), he was placing a bowl of water on top of the toilet door as a booby trap for a teacher. Cecil Amos was often with us too (though he lived in Winforton); cheerful and likeable, Cecil was generally on the lookout for mischief — as most of us were.

I remember one occasion when Desmond Jarrett and I cycled to Kington to see Desmond's mother. The two of us set off for Kington on our made-up bikes on a very hot day, Kington being about five miles away and very much uphill for the first few miles. We had no drinks with us or anything except for an orange, which Desmond had. On reaching the top of Bollingham we stopped for a while, both of us being very hot and thirsty. Desmond never thought twice — he just peeled the orange and gave me half. That's what I call being a pal and I often think of it.

Trevor, Nowt's younger brother, known as 'Popper', liked to tag along with us. We didn't mind, we had fun with him. I remember once Popper wanted to learn to roller skate like the rest of us, and so we decided to give him a training session in our kitchen at Ashcroft. To begin with Popper was like a frozen bird-scarer, and, though he tried hard, after several attempts he had a very sore back-side. After some discussion, we strapped a few cushions round him with belts. 'See how you go now, Pop', we said to him. Of course, taking off across the polished red tiles he was still on the floor in no time at all, but he was soon up, laughing and ready for another go. He went down a good few times, enjoying every moment, but after a while he got the hang of it and was able to go the length of the kitchen and catch the table to steady himself and avoid hitting the wall on the other side. Of course we were all in stitches laughing at Popper's expense, but he didn't mind as it taught him to skate. (The last I heard of Popper was that he was living in Canada with a wife and family, running a hotel.)

Another time we went out and collected rotten eggs. In those days the chickens roamed everywhere and laid in places such as the mangers, the bales of hay and sometimes on the floor in the rickyard. (We knew when the eggs were bad because there were so many in one place that they had obviously not been found by the farmer.) Leaving the barns at Castle Farm, with the eggs shared out amongst us two or three each, we dispersed into two gangs. My gang walked down towards the church and came into the churchyard by the lych-gate and the others came in from the Park Road side.

Once we saw the other gang the fun started. Eggs were going in all directions — when you saw movement you took aim. When I saw Popper raise his head above his gravestone shield I didn't hesitate. I let fly with my ammo, catching Popper full on the forehead. Egg splattered down his face and in his hair. His face was a mixture of surprise and disgust as he emerged from behind the gravestone, looking down in horror at the stinking mess dripping down his front. He kept his mouth firmly shut — for obvious reasons — and the eye on the affected side, but beyond that he just didn't know what to do. Obviously we were going to have to do something.

The smell was overpowering — we couldn't get near him. But we had to get him clean. What we really wanted was a hose-pipe so that we could get him clean without getting close to him but there wasn't a hose-pipe handy. Eventually I said, 'Let's get him to the moat'. So we set off for the castle — keeping our distance from poor Popper! Arriving at the moat we could see it still wasn't going to be an easy job, as we had no brushes, cloths or anything to wash him with. There weren't many volunteers to sort him out but I knew *I* was the one who had created the problem. I took a deep breath and rolled up my sleeves and somehow, by getting Popper to lean forward over the edge of the water and splashing him with our hands, we managed to get the worst off. Then we left him to make for home. To this day I don't know whether his mother ever found out.

From the village it is quite a climb to The Great Oak area but from there you can see a long way. There are lots of lovely views and for me some wonderful memories. Around The Great Oak area as I walk about I often come across things I remember as a young boy — tucked away in the hedgerows here and there an old oven or a box or a bit of drainpipe where the newspapers or goods were left for people to collect … hand water pumps, overgrown by bushes, where people used to collect the water, ideal places now to help wildlife survive. In the road that goes up past The Great Oak, after about a quarter of a mile you come to Newman's Place, where Carmen and Peggy Lloyd now live. This was where Mr Bromage made cider. Nowt and me and a couple of others would often go and watch the men pressing the apples. It was very interesting: I remember that what was left after the juice had been pressed out looked like coconut matting and I remember the smell. We would stay for a while watching the cider-making before making our way on, probably to try making our own or at least help ourselves to a few apples or filberts from the orchards.

From there it is all downhill back to the village — which made it very exciting for us as lads of twelve or thirteen, as we were able to ride our home-made bikes and trucks right down from the highest parts to just past the pump house in the village. (That was on a good day when there was a slight tail wind.) There was very little traffic about then but now and again one met the odd car arriving at the crossroads at the same time as the truck. This called for a quick reaction from the driver of the truck and a loud call to the brake man (sitting backwards). The braking system was his feet being lowered to the ground and pressing down as hard as he could, which was very difficult as our seat was only about a foot wide, so it was more of a balancing act, but thankfully we generally got away with it. What a different story it would be today!

Mind you, there was one occasion when things didn't exactly go according to plan. We had Graham Jones posted as lookout on the other side of the road from the turn-off for The Great Oak. He was all set to give us a signal as we approached the junction to say whether anything was coming down the main road. As was so often the case, I was driving the truck, with several lads behind me, and on this occasion we had managed to achieve tremendous speed. As we came hurtling round the bend with The Great Oak on our left, Graham was gesturing to indicate that nothing was coming and that we could safely turn left to carry on down the hill. Unfortunately I was quite unable to steer a 90° turn at whatever reckless speed we were doing by then. My feeble attempts at warning Graham that he was directly in our path failed completely and we crashed into him and his bike with terrific force. Everybody blamed everybody else for the catastrophe, but nobody was really seriously hurt. But Graham's bike was never the same again.

In the early days in the village we made a lot of our own entertainment — fishing, swimming, skating on frozen ponds or the moat round Eardisley castle, which has a lot of history to it. We explored the woods and surrounding areas, many nights sleeping in the copse by the waterfalls, where quite a few of us learned to swim and catch trout.

Most of us had scrap bikes — bikes we had rescued from dumps. (There were dumps at several places — where there was a hole for some reason — maybe a pool had dried up. There was one at Chennels Gate and another on the right up the Almeley road. We went to the dumps and found all kinds of interesting things that were not in the best of condition — batteries, bikes, spares for bikes, wheels for trucks.) We used our scrap bikes for riding over

'We crashed into him and his bike with terrific force.'

59

rough ground and a favourite place was in the fields adjoining the moat where the sawmills had tipped their sawdust. We would ride down the bank in the field and through the ditches we had made and then crash into the sawdust for a soft landing.

Just round the corner from the copse was the castle moat. This was fed by a brook that also fed the old waterwheel at the mill house, where Mr Morgan lived. The same brook ran down across several fields and was deep enough to swim in, which we often did. The water was not the cleanest of water as, trying to swim between the ducks and the water rats, we stirred the mud up from the bottom. But it was great fun.

Once, when we were about nine, being interested in water and boats we decided to make a boat out of a beer barrel we had found and managed to cut

The Great Oak school 1945–1946. Left to right, back row, Esau Lloyd, Barbara Davies, Florence Jenkins, Brynis Lloyd, Christine Davies, Graham Jones (not more than 100 yards from where he was standing when our home-made truck crashed into him and his bike). Second row, left, Dorothy Cockerell (teacher), John Whittall, Ann Faulkner, right, Olive Jones, David Knights, Ethel Grigg, née Billen, (teacher). Third row, Bobby Davies, Anne Charles, Doreen Vallender, Sam Lloyd, Ann Jones, Kathleen Whittall, Brian Rawlins, Derrick Davies, Denzil Davies, Tommy Jenkins. Front row, David Whittall, Grace Lloyd, Megan Charles, Jean Brookes, Betty Vallender, Colin Hales (my cousin — son of Uncle Jack and Auntie Phyllis who lived in one of the old camp huts. Mrs Grigg told me recently what a lovely singing voice Colin had when he was a little boy.)

in half — I think it came from the castle. It was quite a big barrel so it could hold two or three of us. After a while we had cleaned the barrel out and tidied it up ready for sealing with pitch, which we planned to acquire by collecting old torch batteries and melting them down. This was not very successful — we only managed to get a dribble of something black and sticky. So we had to get some block pitch and melt that as well. Eventually, sealing the barrel, we were ready for launching it on the moat, though the paddles were not the best — they would have been much more suitable to use as walking sticks. It took a while to get going as, having a flat bottom to it and no keel, it was very unstable. It rocked from side to side as the three of us tried to get aboard, but eventually we made it but it was almost impossible to get anywhere because we just kept spinning round in circles. Eventually we gave the barrel boat up but we didn't abandon the idea of building a boat and in later years — with a different design — we had some limited success.

Mr and Mrs Harold Davies farmed Castle Farm at the bottom of the village and brought up a family of four children. As I remember, the times we had at Castle Farm with the children there and other friends were great fun. Mr and Mrs Davies never seemed to mind us playing around in the woods and buildings — in fact I even think they enjoyed us

Aerial view from the church tower looking west, 1960s. On the right are the barns that have now been converted to the houses in Castle Close; at right angles to the barns is a lower building with a dark roof, which was the milking parlour, and in front of that a small white building where the milk was cooled and bottled. On the left, partly obscured by trees, is part of the moat, which, when I was young, completely encircled Castle House, though in places the water ran underground. (I think you can still see some trace of where the moat was today — from the remains of a footbridge — in the woods just behind the Church View houses.) One year, when I was 12 or 13, the moat was frozen over very thick and able to take a lot of weight. I decided (with a little bit of encouragement from the other lads) to take a trip around the moat on our Rudge motorcycle. Nothing too exciting happened — more by luck than judgement — nevertheless, not something to be recommended!

playing there — at least they could keep an eye on us, which, looking back now, was probably a good thing. As we got older we were able to help on the farm in different ways, from driving the tractors to taking the corn to the granary, maybe helping to bring the cows in for milking — there was always so much to be done. After a hard day — as we thought — us boys would visit the outsheds at the farm where we would find a huge barrel of home-made cider with a drinking horn by the side and take drinks. Mr Davies never minded us doing this — I suppose he thought, 'They'll learn'. He was a very nice man — what I would call a 'tidy' man. I will always remember him — sometimes we must have been anything but nice but he always treated us well.

Now and again Mr Davies would have a pig killed at the farm, usually by Mr Edgar Morgan from the watermill house, as he was quite an expert, the family keeping a little butcher's shop. I remember one occasion when Edgar was killing a pig at the back of the castle and he asked for help in holding the pig. This was not too pleasant a thing to do and memories of it still linger on, but, then again, it was food for the house. After the pig was killed there was preparation and cutting up to be done and, as far as I can remember, everything of the pig was used, even its bladder, which us lads used as an inner for our football. The football cover was made of heavy leather, which hurt you if you headed it when it was soaking wet. We used dubbin to waterproof it, and this,

Haymaking in the late 1930s. This picture was taken at Lady Arbour Farm, but it brings back memories of long happy days helping at Castle Farm.

combined with the bladder inside, meant that there was never a very good smell to it — but, then again, we were there to kick the ball, weren't we, not smell it.

We had a lot of fun at Castle Farm. Mr Davies encouraged us to play football, cricket, rounders and tennis, as well as other games. Mr Davies's daughter Olive, now Mrs Olive Morgan and living in Almeley, loved sport, especially tennis, and still does. She has put a lot of enthusiasm into the game in Eardisley, and did so many years ago when the Eardisley tennis courts were grass.

Harvest times were good times. In those days it was binders and thrashing machines. When the corn was being thrashed in front of the barn, the farmer or some of the men would make a makeshift netting fence around the corn bay so that they could catch the rats coming out. Occasionally one might run very close to you, but it was not long before one of the dogs had got it. My own dog, a little terrier named Gyp, who grew up with me, was very popular in the village and a lot of the locals would borrow her to help catch rats or rabbits. Catching rabbits was important: we used to take them home proudly for our mothers to cook — with plenty of sage and onion stuffing they made fine dinners and kept our families going through the war years.

I remember one occasion when Gyp went missing. We were very upset and worried as like most pets she was part of the family and it was hard to take not knowing what had happened to her. But after a few days, when my sister Shirley and I were walking home from school, there she was, this little black and brown terrier, coming down the village at speed to greet us. She was very pleased to see us and we were more than pleased to see her. We found out later that someone had 'borrowed' her for catching rabbits. When Gyp reached her 17th birthday (I was 17 then too because the family had her as a puppy about the time I was born) she was very old and unable to move much and we decided the kindest thing was to call the vet in. I remember watching as he put the needle in to put her to sleep — we were in the old railway carriages at Ashcroft, Dad, the vet, Gyp and me. It was a very sad time as Gyp had been my pal all my life.

In the spring, on most farms there was a lamb — sometimes more than one — that had lost its mother and had to be reared by hand. This made the lambs very close to the ones that fed them and a lot became like pets, following their foster parent like a dog. Mr Harold Davies would often ride his bicycle up to the shop from Castle Farm closely followed by a lamb. My family took in one of these lambs once and fed it using a bottle (maybe a pop bottle) with a proper baby's bottle teat at the end. So I saw at first hand how some of these lambs could behave. We had the lamb from a very early age and had many good times with him, so he became a great pet — we called him 'Larry'. (I expect there were quite a lot of lambs called Larry then!) Larry loved to stand on a slab of concrete that covered the well outside our house and he would butt you if you tried to take his place on the slab. He often visited the garage workshops and nosed around among the bits of engine. He would then be seen coming out, his ears and his curly head severely discoloured, wagging his tail excitedly and chewing bits of rubber inner tube as if they were gum. Sadly, Larry came to the same end as all the other lambs …

Just up the road from the Millennium ground is the Park road and the copse wood where as young lads we had lots of good times. Mostly we had some motorcycle or other, which we had acquired for a couple of pounds or as a swap. On one occasion I made my sister Margaret promise that if I showed her where we had hidden the motorcycle, she wouldn't tell anyone. But I can reveal now where the motorcycle was kept, which was, inside the copse gate by the side of the Home Guard huts, under the hedge, covered in branches and *well* camouflaged. Margaret was very surprised and she *did* keep her promise. We often talk of those times.

One day, down by the moat at the castle, we came across a large dredging machine which they were using to clear out parts of the moat. Looking across the site to where the workmen had left their lunch bags in a hazel tree, we were surprised to see hanging in the tree two or three very large eels which the men had caught in the dredger bucket. I am sure they made a good meal and there must have been plenty more where they came from.

In 1947 I was a young boy going to school in Eardisley. The war was over and gas masks and other wartime things were gradually disappearing — although rationing for most things went on for a long time as things were in very short supply. In the winter the snow fell and kept falling until it got very deep. In some places — such as the Kington and Brilley roads where there was drifting — the snow almost reached up to the telegraph wires. A lot of the country roads and houses were difficult to get to and some people were getting desperate for supplies, but, as in later years, people rallied to the call of others in need. Some farmers with ponies or tractors loaded up with what they could and did their best to keep everyone warm and fed.

With all the difficulties snow caused for adults, my pals and I used to think about the opportunities the snow brought for fun — although in the really bad winter of 1947 the snow was *too* deep for sledging. Red Rasper, designed and built by Nowt, and painted red, was one of our favourite sledges. We took it out onto the snow in the fields at the back of Hollywell Dingle, just along the Almeley road, for trial runs and she turned out to be the best sledge any of us had ridden on — very fast but controllable.

At the bottom of the hill where we were sledging was a brook, which was a sheer drop down from the field above. It was our intention to race down, head first, as fast and as far as we could, often two or three of us together, balancing precariously one on top of another on the narrow sledge. We would leave it to the very last second to dig our toes into the snow or even 'abandon ship' in order to avoid going over the ledge and crashing down into the freezing brook. The inevitable happened a few times, but nobody was seriously hurt, and after a clean-down, and with the brambles and thorns removed, we went on riding the sledges for hours until almost dark. On the way home we 'debriefed', working out how we could improve on performance next time, who had been champion today, who had been the most daring, whether there were any modifications we could do to the runners of the sledge. Our hands and feet and faces must have been wet and cold but in the glow of the afternoon's excitement we hardly noticed. Thinking back on it now, nearly sixty years later, I wonder whether the others remember as vividly as I do the magic of the scene — the snow covering the fields glittering under the bright moonlight, the clear starry sky ...

As the years went by, films began to be regularly shown at the village hall. This was something everyone looked forward to, especially as afterwards the fish and chip van would be waiting at the top of the village. What a wonderful thing it seemed: pictures first, followed by fish and chips! Eardisley film nights started in the 1950s. I think it was Mr Bancroft from Hereford who started them, helped by a local chap called Humphrey Plumstead who was a cinema projectionist in Hereford. Another person who was involved was a Mr Yare from Almeley, and later there was someone else who travelled around with the film shows. Nights varied over the years. Sometimes the pictures were on a Monday night as well as the Saturday, so you would do extra work to get some more pocket money to go again. There was usually a cartoon and a newsreel — *Pathe News*, opening with the crowing cockerell — as well as the main film. Halfway through, sometimes more, the lights would come on in the hall for the projectionist to change the film reel, and the audience often took the opportunity to stretch their legs as the seats were hard. Some of us got into the pictures for nothing by walking in backwards — so they thought we were coming out — but we usually made up for it (or persuaded ourselves that we did) by helping with the equipment. *Great Expectations*, *National Velvet*, *Mother Riley* and *Tarzan* are some of the films I recall, as well as ones featuring Popeye, Laurel and Hardy, and Roy Rogers and his horse, Trigger. Each week posters for the next week's entertainment were put on the local notice boards. There was also a serial featuring a mysterious character called The Scorpion, who wore a mask and had a hooked arm. It went on for some weeks, always leaving you in suspense at the end of the episode. Eventually the mask was removed and the true identity of The Scorpion was revealed.

The story of Genevieve

One of the cars belonging to Mr Oliver Jones's garage was a 1927 16 hp six-cylinder Wolseley — a model known as a 'Silent 6'. She had originally belonged to a Mr Bird, who used to live in a big house on the way to Lower Welson at a place known then as Bird's Pitch (because it was a steep slope). Mr Bird sold the car to a Mr Morris, who ran the Almeley Road garage before Mr Jones. Mr Morris had her converted from a tourer to a saloon car — an excellent job was made of this — and Mr Jones took the car over with the garage, giving her a new lease of life, as she was in for a lot of adventures.

The car had a single-overhead-cam engine and she was a wonderful machine to drive — very unusual, with her 21-inch wheels, 4-speed, gate-change gearbox (which I think was in reverse order) and the accelerator pedal between the clutch and the foot-brake. (No wonder she left the road now and again!) Coachbuilt, with leather seats, she was full of character. She had a six-volt electric system but her battery was not very good and her starter motor was tired. So to get her going we had to swing the handle at the bottom of the radiator round again and again until the magneto fired. Then the engine came to life and ticked over like a watch. Very square and upright, with plenty of room inside, wide running boards, and a large carrying rack at the rear, she could carry a lot of equipment, which later came in useful when we went off camping. She had automatic windows — the first I had ever seen: you could pull the windows down to the required level and then lock them in position by pulling a brass ring; when you released the ring as they were spring-loaded the windows went back up. She also had blinds on the rear windows and built-in hand grips to hold on to going round corners. Somehow she seemed to me the sort of car Laurel and Hardy would have travelled in.

When we were getting on for the age when we could legally drive, one or two of us got interested in getting the Wolseley on the road, and we eventually did this in 1954. The year before a film (starring Kenneth More and Kay Kendall) featuring veteran cars had been a great success and it was probably this that inspired us to give the Wolseley the name Genevieve. (The Genevieve in the film was a 1904 Darracq and so qualified as a veteran — pre-1905 — but our vehicle was just inside the age range for a vintage car — 1919 to 1930.) Our car got called other things from time to time. 'Vacuum' because of the … er … bits of fluff she picked up! 'Rolls-Can-Hardly' (Rolls down one hill, Can Hardly get up the next) because at one stage she could hardly roll, especially if water had got into the vacuum tank (which delivered fuel to the carburettor). Often we'd be stuck at the side of the road with the bonnet up and one of us cleaning the

Genevieve — largely obscured by (left to right) Derry Barker (on his BSA B31), Keith Needes, Graham Jones, Ronnie Barker and me (on the BSA 250 cc I bought from Keith and repaired after he crashed it) — mid-Fifties

water out of the tank. But then, with a bit of luck and a swing of the starting handle, away we'd go.

I remember one occasion when we'd gone to a sale at Broxwood. Afterwards we all piled back into Genevieve. There would have been Nick, Nowt, Graham Jones and Roy Thomas, besides me, and probably one or two others as well, and I remember it was my turn to drive home. I set off down a long narrow drive surrounded by trees and beautiful lawns. It was a one-way road, with an 'In' and an 'Out', and so when I started up I didn't expect to meet anything coming the other way. Soon the lads were shouting for me to go faster and I went up to top gear, my foot flat down on the accelerator, doing all of 30 mph. Suddenly a green Rover 75 was heading straight at us. It was quite a posh car and I really didn't want to hit it. So the only option was to make for the high laurel hedge running the full length of the drive. Through the hedge we went, leaving a large hole, and Genevieve came to an abrupt halt against a six-bar gate. Steam was streaming skywards, as were the front mudguard and the running board, and the temperature gauge on top of the radiator was going mad. The lads in the back were laughing as the posh lady driver of the Rover approached us: 'I've never seen such incompetent driving in all my life!' she said. 'I'm very sorry, I think my foot must have stuck to the accelerator', I said feebly, wishing I had the courage to ask whether she hadn't seen the 'No Entry' sign. The posh lady stormed off and we never heard any more from her. I suppose if Genevieve had had better brakes it might have helped — but I still think she should have seen that sign, especially as I think she was the owner of the house.

There was a real art to driving Genevieve and it sometimes needed a team effort. Night-driving of course meant that the headlights had to be dipped to oncoming traffic. (The full power of Genevieve's headlights was about equivalent to the light of a small torch but the headlights still had to be dipped.) To dip the lights the driver had to reach down to his right side and pull on a lever. This in turn pulled a long bar that ran across the side of the car and was attached at the front to another bar to which the headlights were fixed on a hinge. When the driver pulled the lever the hinge made the lights go up or down, but the dipping mechanism, like the brakes, was a bit slow. So, when Genevieve went out at night everyone looked out for oncoming traffic and at the first sign of approaching lights a chorus would go up 'Dip!'

I remember one occasion when we set off on an exciting trip to camp in Porthcawl. The car was loaded up using every available bit of space, the kit bags between the front wings and the engine, the tents on the roof rack, and all the kitchen utensils crammed into the large rear carrier. And inside, of course, was the usual gang, with Nowt driving. Derry Barker and I rode our motorcycles, escorting Genevieve. We passed through several villages on the way, one, at the bottom of a steep hill. Sometimes, after a long downhill run, Genevieve would get a build-up of smoke in the engine and this would come belching forth when the throttle was opened again. As we neared a stone bridge entering this village, we saw some men who looked as if they might have been miners. Some were leaning against the bridge and some were sitting on it, and (until we arrived) they appeared to be just sitting around and talking casually, in their white silk scarves, peaked caps and wide-bottomed trousers. But at the sight of Genevieve they looked up in amazement! An elderly saloon car filled to bursting with camping gear and a bunch of high-spirited lads, followed by two motor-cyclists, and everything enveloped in clouds of smoke — I expect it was a change from what they usually saw as they chatted together at the bridge.

We found more spectators as we drew near to the camp site on the outskirts of Porthcawl and discovered we had unwittingly joined a carnival procession. We went along with this for a while and the crowd seemed to think we were part of the show but at the first opportunity to escape we broke loose to find our camp site. We pitched our tent at Rest Bay by a stone wall. This sheltered us from the wind and rain but also seemed to make the spot an ideal one for snakes. One morning, as the sun was warming up and I was outside washing, I saw a snake just a yard or so from the tent. It didn't take much notice of me and I think it was just a grass snake, but at the age we were then we found it a little worrying to know we were sleeping so close to snakes, especially as our tent was not in the best condition.

Another day, during a wet spell, we found our food supplies were getting very low — we were down to one packet of custard, in fact. Getting more food meant going off to Porthcawl in Genevieve, but the heavy rain was showing up leaks in the tent. So it was decided that Nick and myself would stay behind and make sure everything was all right inside the tent and the other lads would go off to the shops, hoping no water would get into Genevieve's fuel system. After a long time we began to wonder where the lads had got to — not that we could do much about it. But knowing Nowt was there was reassuring as we knew he'd be able to fix anything that might have gone wrong. By this time Nick and myself felt very hungry as we had not had any breakfast and it was now about lunch time. After a little discussion we made up the packet of custard. We thought we ought to make as much as we could in case the other lads wanted some. So we used the last drop of milk — and some water. We were glad they did not want any of the custard when they eventually returned with food supplies. There wasn't much left — and it was awful! Later the weather improved and we all piled into Genevieve to go to the fair in Porthcawl for a good night out. So at least the day ended well.

We had a lot of fun touring the local lanes with Genevieve — doing a lot of ditching along the way and Eardisley people always waved and smiled as Genevieve went through the village, but eventually National Service intervened, bringing an end to these adventures. I often wonder where Genevieve is today. Good times.

Chapter Six: Village Life

There were two Miss Gwatkins, Miss Gertie and Miss Lilian Gwatkin. (I am not sure which one this is a picture of, but I think it is Gertie.) My father always took a lump of coal into their house at midnight on New Year's Eve.

Eardisley laundry

In Eardisley village in the 1930s and 1940s laundry was taken in at Stoneleigh, which is situated next to the village shop in the middle of the village. The washing was done in part of the house and then put through the mangle. It was then dried on a long line in the garden. The ironing was done in the outhouse — with irons heated on fires until later on the more modern electric irons came in. As young lads we found the outhouse where the ironing was done a very good place for making our home-made elderberry and damson 'wine'. I don't think anybody drank it, mind. It was more like sour soup than wine! Although the laundry has long since finished, memories of it linger on. Miss Emily Parsons, who bought Stoneleigh and started the laundry, employed a few local people, including Mrs Arrowsmith, Mrs May Thomas and Mrs Milward. Sadly some of these have passed on and Miss Parsons herself died in 1955 aged 69 years. There used to be a few other people in the village who took laundry in too, including the two Miss Gwatkins, who lived in The Old House, next door to Mr Thomas Burgoyne, the blacksmith. I don't know when laundries like these finished but as time went on other services started, with the laundry being picked up and collected by vans. And, of course, more and more people bought washing machines.

Tom and Maggie Louise Morgan — Wilf Morgan's shop

In Eardisley there were several unconnected Morgan families. One of these was the family of Tom and Maggie Louise Morgan, who lived at the water mill at the bottom of the village. They had ten children: Phyllis, Elsie, Mona, Margery, Jack, Trevor, Edgar, Wilfred, Victor and Cyril (confusingly known as *Jim* Morgan). I didn't know them well and when I was a boy most of them had got married and left home. Wilfred (Wilf) had a little shop at the side of the main road and Tom would often be seen, in his trilby hat and carrying his forked stick, walking across the field to the shop. Before my time Wilf (and his father before him) had run this as a butcher's shop. Sometime in the Thirties the family decided to change their business and they went into wool, knitting patterns, nylons (even when they were rather hard to come by), baby-wear and, I think, probably ladies' underwear. But as well as these things they sold pencils, rubbers, rulers … all kinds of stationery, birthday cards, and then sweets — some of them in tall thick jars with heavy glass tops on the shelves at the back of the shop — bull's-eyes, barley sugar, humbugs, lollipops, gobstoppers, chewing gum and bubble gum, Nippets (tiny black squares of liquorice in packets — and, I think, tins as well). Wilf sold snuff too. During the war Wilfred went away to the forces so his wife, Muriel, ran the shop. Some things were on ration but it was good to have the shop there all the same. When Wilfred came home he took over the shop again, but things were still rationed and I vividly

Wilfred Morgan's shop about 1950. Back in the early Thirties it had been a butcher's shop. Standing in front are Wilf and Muriel Morgan with their daughter, Thelma.

Snuff

Snuff came in little round aluminium tins about 1¼" across and about ½" deep. You got at the contents by sliding open a tiny aperture in the side and tapping out what you wanted onto the thumb side of the back of the hand. Taking snuff was very common almost into the Seventies. I remember my grandfather and a good many of his friends enjoyed it. It wasn't just men who used it, but they certainly used it more than women, and, while men of all sorts used it, it was unusual to see a 'lady' take snuff.

remember how if we went to buy sweets he would cut out of our ration books our last few monthly coupons until the next month's issue. (In fact I didn't actually buy sweets much; usually I sold my sweet coupons to my brother — it was quite a hard decision to make, money or sweets, but mostly I went for the money — a lovely, solid, heavy 12-sided threepenny bit.)

Mr and Mrs Wilf Morgan lived the other side of the road from their shop. I remember watching them climb over a stile beside a six-barred gate and make their way, past grazing animals, along the well worn path that ran diagonally across a small field — in summer it was always full of buttercups and daisies, lady's-smock, clover — all sorts of wildflowers. At the end they had to go over a narrow wooden footbridge; as children, we found its springiness exciting as we deliberately clomped across, but I don't suppose Wilfred and his wife felt the same way and I would imagine they would have appreciated the handrails. At the end of the bridge they had another stile to cross, and this one took them to their black-and-white cottage beside the brook.

Today it's all entirely different: Hadley Rill — Shân's shop — stands where Wilf's shop was; Joyce Banbury's front garden is where the stile and the big gate were; and the bouncy bridge has gone, though there are just faint traces of where it once was at the edge of Jenny and Anthony Davis's garden. And, if you look carefully the other side of the stream at that point, you can just make out — at least I can — something suggesting where the bridge went into the bank and where the stile was. But it's all overgrown and most signs of what was there have been obliterated. Millstream Gardens are very nice but quite a change from the lovely field of my childhood, with the sheep and ponies.

Tom Burgoyne the blacksmith

When I was young the village blacksmith was Mr Thomas Burgoyne, a well-built man but not tall, with a moustache. He shoed horses and did general metal-work, mostly with the hand-blown bellows, in a shop adjoining his house and close to the village hall.

Some of the horses were quite big, the carthorses in particular, and they could be very lively when being shoed but Mr Burgoyne always managed to get the job done. He tied the horse up and then lifted up a hoof and rested it between his legs on his leather apron. First he cleaned the hoof ready to take the shoe. Meanwhile the fire would be being fanned by the long-handled bellows, sometimes by one of the youngsters. As the flames got hotter the shoe begin to glow red-hot. Then it was put to the horse's hoof to make sure it fitted properly: it would burn into the hoof, the smoke and the smell of burnt hoof would rise and Mr Burgoyne would move his head from side to side to avoid the smoke. None of this seemed to affect the horses — certainly they felt no pain from the hot metal. Sometimes one of the horses played up and then the whites of Mr Burgoyne's eyes would show as he sensed trouble brewing. But before long he would have sorted out the problem.

The blacksmith's shop was a wonderful place to visit. We loved to watch while he shoed the horses and worked away with the metals. Sometimes he might be fitting metal rims to wooden cartwheels first heating up the rims and then shrinking them once they were on the wheel by dousing them with cold water from a barrel in the yard. Sometimes he would be banging his large hammer sharply down on the anvil and causing the sparks to fly — as they did in more ways than one if Mr Burgoyne was annoyed.

Sheep being driven through the village in the 1950s — a Ford 8 (or Ford 10) van has stopped to let the sheep through. Notice the fencing all along the road — there were hardly any driveways into people's gardens then.

He was tolerant to us lads, as we were often around and probably in his way a lot of the time. Sometimes we would go to him with a pig's bladder and ask him if he would fit it inside a worn-out football case and blow it up for us. He did this without hesitation, as he loved anything to do with football, being captain of Eardisley football team and teaching football at Eardisley school. He also ran a little village library from the blacksmith's shop, lending out books mainly on the Wild West, I think.

As years went by and horses began to be used less, Mr Burgoyne started to sell bicycles and towards the end of the 1940s Harry, Mr Burgoyne's elder son, began looking around with his father for a garage to set up business in the motor trade. Sadly, Mr Tom Burgoyne died on 16th December 1950 at the age of 66, (two years after his wife, Amy), before his sons were able to find anywhere for the garage. Harry carried on with some of his father's unfinished business, and in 1953 his brother Doug joined him, and together they ran the blacksmith's and a bicycle shop — Central Cycle Stores, selling Raleigh, Hercules and BSA cycles. Gradually they developed the garage side of the business, using Mr Dennis Sharples's premises in the centre of the village as a repair workshop.

After some time the Burgoyne brothers decided to build in the orchard next to where Mr Brierley the butcher's shop was (Ye Olde House — where Jean and Arthur Franklin live). They built up a very successful business, which their sons, Roger and Douglas Junior, took over when they died and it is only recently that the premises have been sold.

Across the main road from The Wharf Eardisley now has a new blacksmith — Simon Ashby. It is so good to see a blacksmith back in the village. His work is of a very high standard and he carries out a lot of traditional blacksmith's work — a real joy to see.

The village hall

The village hall — the Curzon Herrick Hall, to give it its proper name — was built in about 1900, but it has served the village well. During the war years plays, whist drives, dinners and youth club meetings took place there, as well as dances with live bands. The Diamond Players, The Legionnaires and The Golden Linnets played at various times; there was also a band with almost all women players led by a Mrs Jay from the shop at Winforton.

The caretaker's house — known as The Institute — was next to the hall and the caretaker and his wife, Mr and Mrs Rowland Webb, sold pop there — I remember seeing the wooden crates outside in which the bottles had been delivered. We sometimes stopped to buy a glass of pop on the way home from school — we had to knock on the front door — and after the drinks had been poured out I remember the bottles being resealed with a flip-top. I think when Mrs Webb was selling it to us the pop cost about three old pennies a glass or 'thra-punce', as we would have said then. We could not afford it often but enjoyed a glass now and then. My favourite — and most children's — was the red (cherry flavour) pop. The best times were when I could have a packet of crisps as well!

Just across the road from the village hall is the one and only remaining grocer's shop, which has been there as long as I can remember. The other shops that were in Eardisley in my childhood have long gone. I first knew the village shop as Triffitt's. They baked bread there then — two men called Mr Gale and Mr Jenkins baked it in the back of the shop. The shop supplied a lot of bread in those days — I remember boys from The Holme (the house at the top of the village right on the junction with the Almeley road) loading up a two-wheeled wooden handcart with bread from Triffitt's to take back for the many lads who were staying there. It was lovely bread — sometimes when I was sent across to the shop for a loaf I would arrive back home with only three-quarters of it as it was so good to eat, nice and fresh and warm, not long out of the ovens. My mother would have a few words with me about it, but I couldn't help it if there were a lot of mice about, could I?

Mr and Mrs Napper Davies
There were a few places in Eardisley where you could buy pop and crisps and different things. The shop at the bottom of the village was an old railway carriage — two carriages put together actually, living quarters and a shop — set in a small part of an orchard and surrounded by apple trees. Children would often call in there for pop and sweets on the way home from school. Mr George Davies and his wife Edith (Mr and Mrs Napper Davies) ran the shop and were nice to everyone but especially the children who shopped there. I remember they had a tall round cage, with a dome on the top and a large door in front, with a tame jackdaw in it. This was outside behind the carriages and we often used to go round and look at it and talk to it as this was something very unusual. I think they tried to teach it to talk — and it did to a point. Looking back it seems cruel to keep a bird in a cage, but things were different then —

we collected birds' eggs and butterflies and put all sorts of little creatures in jam jars. Some things over time have changed for the better.

Mr Davies was always called Napper Davies — and sometimes 'Napper Davies the carriages'. Some people think that this name suggests that he or one of his forbears worked as a 'knapper', someone who breaks large pieces of stone down into smaller stones, which used to be done by hand. I don't know if this is the case but I do know that at one time Mr and Mrs Davies lived at Knapp House at the top of the village. Later, they and their family went to live in the two railway carriages, which were quite good accommodation. The carriages had been delivered to the orchard site by horse and

Janet Davies's newsagent's shop just before it closed in May 2003. Shân Sherwood is buying a newspaper from Janet.

timber carriage by Mr Bert Hammond, who in those days worked as a timber haulier for Mr Spearman, who owned the mill by the present doctor's surgery. Sadly, the carriages were dismantled round about the 1950s. A bungalow called Orchardville, where Tony and Pat Lane live, is now on the site.

Mr Brierley the butcher

In what is now Jean and Arthur Franklin's house, next door to the garage that was formerly Burgoyne's, was one of the local butcher's shops — Mr Brierley's. When I was very young Mr Brierley still used a pony and trap to deliver the meat — a very high trap, almost like a stagecoach. (At least, that is how it appeared to me in those days.) Occasionally I used to go on the round with the driver of the horse, doing the deliveries. The meat was inside the box-like trap and we sat high above it and so, as I was not very big then, I had difficulty climbing back up onto the top after giving someone their parcel of meat. One day the driver was negotiating Hobby Lyons bridge as he drove towards the village returning from a delivery. We were travelling at quite a pace when the

H W Smith & Son, the butcher's at 1 Church Road before Mr Brierley, probably in the early Thirties. The building further up the road in this picture, the cider house, was demolished in about 1960 to allow development of the site of Burgoyne's garage. The trap that Mr Brierley used for meat delivery had big wheels like the ones in this picture. When the accident happened at Hobby Lyons bridge when I was 'helping' deliver the meat, the hub of one of the wheels caught on a stone pillar as Ken Emins (Hemmings?) tried to turn a sharp corner too quickly. Mr Brierley's trap was much higher than this one, much more like a stagecoach, so I was thrown from a long way up. It is astonishing really that I was not injured in the fall, or even killed.

large hub of the trap caught the stone pillar and in a split second I was thrown off the trap down onto the road. I was quite shaken up, but thankfully not hurt too badly, and when I eventually got back on the trap we made back for home very steadily. If I remember correctly I didn't deliver any more meat with *that* pony and trap.

When I was some years older, one night in early November we were going down past the shop while Mr Brierley was cutting the meat up for next day. Not realising the damage it might do, one of the lads put a firework through the metal ventilators. (Looking back now, this was a very stupid thing to do: Mr Brierley could have been injured and the firework fumes certainly did spoil the meat.) The next thing we knew Mr Brierley and the local policeman were after us as the firework had gone off in the shop. They never caught us though, as everyone had disappeared into the night fields and sat it out until the coast was clear and I don't think anything more was done about it. I do hope that Mr Brierley forgave us all for what happened. The bigger boys made up a little song about it —

Here comes Brierley with a rusty knife
Doodah, doodah
Here comes Brierley with a rusty knife
Doo, doodah, day

Brierley, Brierley, shall I die?
Doodah, doodah …

Mr William Brierley. Mr Brierley was a quiet, usually serious man, who ran his butcher's business well and was a leading member of the congregation of the Methodist chapel. He was one of the regulars on the bowling green at the rectory.

Maybe someone will remember a bit more of it than I can — it was quite popular at the time.

The cobbler's shop — Dick Webb

Before being a cobbler's (but long before my time) the little building next to Povey's had been a butcher's. Looking around at the shop you could see this, as meat hooks still hung from the ceiling, Dick's wooden workbench had a tiled top, and the well-worn cobbler's last on which he placed shoes for repair work was fixed to a wooden butcher's block alongside the workbench.

The shop wasn't very big — about 9 feet square — and as you went in, on your right, behind the heavy-duty sewing machine, was a shelf where Dick kept his polishes, dyes, threads, brushes, etc. On the left were shelves of repaired shoes waiting for collection, and sometimes bridles and saddles. Quite often Dick had his bicycle (occasionally even his motorbike) leaning against it. The workbench was to your right, with Dick facing you behind it. Sheets of leather of different sizes and varying thicknesses were arranged like packs of cards just below a small window at the rear of the shop, and above the sewing machine were several long-out-of-date calendars. Beside these old calendars hung the latest pin-up, which went down well with a lot of the chaps. The walls and the shop window were usually full of posters and notices that people had asked Dick to put up for different village functions. He always agreed to put these notices up even though it made it difficult to see out of the window, but Dick was always willing to please and never grumbled. He also kept a small mirror on the wall, to check that he was clean and tidy before leaving the premises, as he was always very particular about his appearance.

Stephen Hatcher standing in front of Dick Webb's cobbler's shop in the early Fifties

Full of character, with its sturdy old fittings and its smells of leather, polishes and dyes, Dick's shop was a wonderful little place. People, including the postman and the policeman, regularly called in to warm their hands and feet in the winter and have a chat with Dick while he carried on busily working. His tools and his body both showed signs of the wear they'd had over the years: there were indentations where he had held his tools and where long use had worn them away, and his knuckles were swollen. Rather strangely, the ends of his ears seemed to have been worn too, from his habit of spitting on his hands and brushing back his hair with his fingers before hammering in a nail. Now and again Dick stopped for a blow and joined in the conversation. He liked talking football and other sport.

Many of my evenings were spent with my pals in Dick's warm little workshop, which smelt of paraffin, watching him work — I can see him now, sitting there holding nails in his mouth. We were probably a nuisance but Dick never seemed to mind. I watched fascinated as he knocked nails into boots and shoes, stitched school satchels and sharpened his knife on a leather strap or a stone. I watched him select a piece of leather from the pile and carefully mark, cut and fit it. And then I watched as he finished off by giving the leather a good polish. Dick always had plenty of work and always did his best to get it done by the time he had promised to have it ready for collection — he gave Eardisley and Almeley an excellent service over many years.

Dick also had a small place at Almeley, just across the road from Almeley church, and once or twice a week he would cycle over to work there. He some-

Tram Square showing the timber stables pulled down in the 1960s. They had not been used as stables for some time but I remember seeing horses looking out from the stable half-doors at this end of the building when I was a little boy. I think the horses then belonged not to The Tram but to local farmers. Just in front of the Arboyne House end of the stable is a cast-iron signpost for Woodseaves, Almeley, Kington and probably Hereford. Outside The Tram the ground was paved with cobbles about three yards into the square from the building. The buses all parked here to pick passengers up to go to Hay, Hereford and Kington and youngsters gathered here on Sunday afternoons when they had nothing else to do. Sometimes we played pitch and toss in what we called the wain house, which is still there, up the side of The Tram, and sometimes we would amuse ourselves with carbide, setting off little explosions. Carbide was a chalky material sold (in cylindrical tins about 2" in diameter and 7" long) for use in cycle lamps. You drilled a hole in one end of an empty tin and put inside it a small piece of carbide with a drop of water. Then you put the lid on, shook the tin a bit (you could hear fizzing inside) and put the tin on the ground with your foot firmly on it. At the last minute you put a lighted match to the hole you'd drilled, there would be a big bang and the tin lid would shoot to the other side of the square!

View of Tram Square when Mr Baird was landlord of The Tram in the 1930s. Dick Webb's cobbler's shop can just be seen against the end wall of Arboyne House. As you can see there were lots of advertising signs on the side of the shop. You can see the wall and the hedge round The New Inn in this picture too.

times went on his Francis Barnet motorbike (which was exactly like the one my sister and I are sitting on in the picture on the front cover of this book), but I remember him more with his pushbike — at least that's how I see him in my mind at the end of a day, locking up his shop and getting on his bike to ride home down through the village. He lived with his mother at the bottom of the village, next to the fire station, in a house that has now been knocked into one with the adjoining house and called The White House. He took a keen interest in bowls at the rectory garden and he liked a game of billiards. Now and again he enjoyed a walk along the lanes or around the village fields and generally relaxing from his work.

In later years, with modern ways of doing things, there was less work for him and when he finally retired Eardisley lost a lovely character. Dick's little workshop was used after he retired by a Mr Morrish for making up stained glass windows. Later it was taken down altogether. Dick died at the age of 73 on 1st August 1980.

I am sure the world was put right many times, and definitely a lot of football was played beside the stoves in the village shops of my young days. On cold days people often called in to different places where there was a stove — they were almost like meeting points — I remember my father's garage with its tortoise stove — people often came and stood by that. Some of the stories got a little exaggerated now and then; some of the things it was hard to imagine — like when a football had been kicked so hard it stuck in the corner at the top of the

Houses at Hobby Lyons in the 1940s. My Hales grandparents lived here from about 1952 until they died. My great uncle, Jim Marshall, and his wife, Auntie Becky, lived in the house on the left and some people called Jenkins lived in the house on the right. The wooden railings on the wooden footbridge in the foreground have now been replaced with metal ones

goalpost. Other stories were fascinating, such as the one where a gentleman jumped into crocodile-infested waters to save the life of someone who had fallen in: a third person immediately threw his cap into the crocodile's mouth and saved both the people in the water. (I take my cap off to him there!)

Bob Wynne the butcher
Just a few doors up from Triffitt's (in the shop that until recently was Janet Davies's newsagents) was one of the Eardisley butcher's shops, Bob Wynne's. Povey's butcher's shop had been there for many years before. The shop delivered meat all round the area by van or cycle, each order with a label pinned on to it, showing the customer's name and the price of the meat, with a little metal pin specially for that job. At the back of the premises animals were slaughtered. Mr Wynne himself — Bob Wynne — was a very big man. Most people in the area knew him because he was a quite a character. He was a very good dancer and every New Year's Eve ran a dance in the village hall. It was known as Bob Wynne's Dance and everyone looked forward to it. The hall floor was dusted thickly with a white chalk-like powder that made dancing easier and Mr Wynne always dressed for the occasion in a very nice black evening suit and tie. Not long after things had got underway, however, for some unknown reason Mr Wynne's lovely black suit would be covered in white powder. The village ladies

would all want to start the evening with a dance with Mr Wynne, but I think he really should have been dancing with just one lady at a time. He didn't seem to mind if his dancing partners got in the way of both his feet at the same time and he didn't seem to take much time to reach the floor! It *did* seem to take a while for him to get *up* on his feet again, as his dancing partners, who were helping him up, could hardly see for tears of laughter. He just dusted himself down and took it all as fun — I think he loved every minute of it. That's how I remember him.

Charlie Carter the electrician

Above Mr Jarrett's house in later years was a shop owned by Mr and Mrs Eric Clark, which sold newspapers and other things. On the opposite side of the road, lived Mr and Mrs Charlie Carter. Mr Carter was an electrician and had a little electrical shop. The shop, which was adjacent to the south side of the house, was a wooden-framed shed, about 10' by 6' by 6', with large windows in the top half, displaying torches, batteries, plugs, etc. There was another little building at the side of the garage, which was on the north side of the house, in which Mr Carter charged accumulators for customers. There was a big table inside and the accumulators would be lined up on it, all labelled with their

The Common road, showing the Cruck House with a glasshouse. This picture looks quite old but the glasshouse was still there when I was a boy. It was used not to grow things in but as a conservatory. I remember that the people who lived there then (they were called Dawkins) had an Opel car — which was quite unusual — we did not often see German cars. Mrs Dawkins may have been Swedish — she was certainly blonde and pretty.

owners' names. Sometimes you might go in to collect your accumulator and Mr or Mrs Carter would tell you that it wasn't ready — it hadn't yet been charged. But this wasn't really a problem because they'd say to you, 'Well, here's Mr Jones's. It's done. Do you mind taking his instead?' (And later, when Mr Jones came for his, he might be given yours — or someone else's. But they were all labelled, so they didn't get muddled!) Mr Carter was a very friendly person, always ready to help. When I worked in Hay-on-Wye, if ever my motorbike was out of action Mr Carter was always happy to give me a lift in the back of his little Ford van in amongst the coils of cable and his tools.

Povey's

Povey's shop, at the top of the village in Arboyne House, was the grocer's where as lads we went to get broken biscuits free before going down the lanes or across the fields eating them — the shop keepers were good to the youngsters in the village then (as I am sure they are now). Next to Povey's and adjoining it was Richard Webb's cobbler's shop in a small wooden building. When this was demolished some years later, the following words were discovered, which had been hidden on the wall behind:

Noted House
For Best Quality
Goods At Store Prices
For Cash

Today this writing can be seen on the end wall of Arboyne House.

Miss Leake

Miss Leake lived with her mother and sister, Harriet, at The Duke's, along Bower Lane, where Sonia Taylor lives now. Both sisters may have worked at the post office — what I clearly remember was that Miss *Elizabeth May* Leake used to deliver the post around Eardisley area on a bicycle. She walked with a very marked stoop — probably due to some medical condition — and when she rode her bicycle she always seemed to be looking down rather than ahead, so she did not look too safe, but I am sure she was. She was well respected for carrying out her job well, pedalling round her considerable delivery area in all weathers, with the

Miss Elizabeth May Leake — considering the fact that she had an elderly mother to look after and that her job was demanding with regard to weather conditions, especially in winter time, Miss Leake seemed to me to be someone who made the most of life.

George Morgan's wood mill (on the site where the surgery is now) after the fire in the early Thirties. Frank Morgan, now in his 80s and living near the tennis courts, can be seen here as a boy of about ten.

letters in a large post-office bag. Sometimes the odd person might report that the post was late. What they did not realize was that some kind person had called Miss Leake in for a warm and a cup of tea. But as far as I know, though she would accept the tea and have a little talk, she stayed on the doorstep.

She seemed to enjoy supporting the Eardisley Sports and Carnival and used to push her mother along in a wheelchair in the carnival procession, with herself, the older lady and the wheelchair all in carnival dress, often flowers. They usually won a prize. After her mother died Miss Leake kept up her carnival tradition, decorating her bicycle instead of the wheelchair. Long after she retired she would still often be seen riding her bicycle to Kington.

Eardisley station
When I was about ten or eleven, the sound of the trains coming into Eardisley station was something I looked forward to at regular times of the day. I still remember the sound and smell of them. Sometimes we would go down to the station and look over the bridge and watch the trains going under, the smoke from the train billowing up into our faces. Occasionally we would take a trip on the train to Hay-on-Wye or to Hereford, depending on how much pocket money we had earned.

A train ran from Hereford to Brecon, calling at all the small stations — Credenhill, Moorhampton, Kinnersley, Eardisley, Whitney, Hay-on-Wye, Glasbury, Three Cocks, Talgarth and Tallynflyn — on the way. On the return journey it called at all the same stops. There was also a private stop on the Foxley estate near Credenhill, where they put a flag out if they wanted the train to halt.

Dick Brookes, 1950s. Mr Richard Brookes, who was an agent for a coal company in South Wales, started a business as a coal merchant in Eardisley in the late 1920s. He lived with his wife and children, including Dorothy (now Dorothy Joseph) and Doreen (now Doreen Payne) at The Wharf, near Eardisley station, where the coal arrived by rail. For many years he delivered coal with a horse and cart around the village and the outlying areas, talking to one and all as he went on his rounds — it was a part of village life. He was the first coalman I remember in Eardisley and he carried on the business until he retired in 1954.

As well as these passenger services there were freight trains, such as the fish trains and the liquid tanker trains, which kept the sidings busy unloading materials, coal and other things. There was also the main weighbridge at the station where trucks and trailers could be weighed. On the platforms there were machines for a variety of purposes, from ones where you could print your name on an aluminium strip to chocolate machines (empty, of course, because of wartime rationing). I am sure a lot of people remember talking by the fireside as they sat in the waiting room waiting for their trains — there was always something to talk about.

In the early Sixties, when Dr Beeching was making his savage cuts to the railway system, parts of the station were dismantled. Some, such as the booking office, which went to somewhere near Welshpool, were taken to other local stations and rebuilt, which is nice to know as the station has many memories for Eardisley people. There was something about those days, the trains, the sound of the whistle, the steam, the energy and the activity at the bottom of the village. I am sure we all miss it.

Mr Sidney Jones
After Richard Brookes retired, the coal business was taken over by Mr Walter
Howells and his partner, Mr Sidney Jones, and the coal began to be delivered
by lorries. Mr Jones was the one mainly involved in the coal side of the business
and he ran it very well; it was hard work unloading the coal from the railway
trucks, weighing it off into sacks by hand and later carrying the sacks — sometimes a long way — up garden paths or up steps. Mr Jones was the sort of man
who just got on with things. In 1990, some time after he retired, Mr Jones and
his wife moved from their house at The Turn down to Orchard Close.

The Fire Service
At various times this has been called the National Fire Service, the Auxiliary
Fire Service, the Hereford Fire Brigade and the Hereford and Worcester Fire
Brigade. When I was a lad in 1947 it was called the NFS — National Fire
Service. The fire engine was a so-called ATV — Austin Towing Vehicle —
towing a Dennis pump and the Eardisley members of the service were Sub
Officer Billy Nicholas and Leading Fireman Ken Townsend, along with Jack
Moulton, Gerald Hales, Arthur Prosser and Glyn Jones. Sub Officer Nicholas
died suddenly at the early age of 60 in 1959 and Leading Fireman Ken
Townsend took over. When he retired the present Sub Officer, Chris Davies,
took over.

The opening of the new fire station in Eardisley by Mr A V Thomas, HM Inspector of
Fire Brigades, in 1966. This picture shows the demonstration of fire fighting local
firemen gave for the visitors. My father, Gerald Hales, who had just retired from twenty
years in the Retained Fire Service, was presented on this occasion with the Fire Brigade
Long Service and Good Conduct Medal by the chairman of the fire Brigade Committee,
Alderman W D Porter.

In Billy Nicholas's time the pump was detachable from the fire engine and so the fire crew were able to sit in the back of the ATV behind canvas curtains that pulled across to act as doors. As the fire engine in those days was stationed at Modello Works garage, it was easily accessible and very close to the village hall, and the curtained-off area at the back became a favourite place for courting couples. I think many a glow started there. In the days when Sub Officer B Nicholas was in charge of Eardisley Brigade the firemen would parade on certain days for practice and cleaning the equipment. At night, if there was a fire, the call would come through to Sub Officer Nicholas, who would in turn call the other firemen by means of a bell system which he would ring by winding a handle on a special piece of equipment in his home. Later, when Sub Officer Townsend took over, the alarm system had improved. In 1956 a siren for daytime call-outs was fitted at the Modello Works Fire Station. This was used for some years until again the system was improved; this time the firemen were issued with small pocket phones to carry with them at all times. But even with these there could be the occasional problem, such as when one of the firemen lost his phone whilst out walking. The only way anyone could think of to find it again was for all the other firemen to be warned to ignore a call at a certain time. Then the one who had lost his phone went back to where he thought he had lost it and listened to hear where the sound of the call was coming from.

There were times when there was a fire somewhere in a remote area and the firemen had problems finding their way to it. Once it was decided to pick up one of the crew from his home as he knew the area very well, being one of the local roadmen. When the fire engine arrived he came running out to meet the rest of the crew half dressed, struggling with his uniform and with kit going everywhere. But he jumped aboard and successfully navigated the fire engine and crew to the fire and they were able to do their job and extinguish the fire.

Another time when they were trying to locate a fire one of the fireman said, 'We must be somewhere near the fire, as I can smell burning'. The fire the fireman could smell at that moment was indeed very near: the wiring of the fire engine had caught alight! Fortunately it wasn't long before the crew realized what had happened and extinguished the fire on board before going on to deal with the fire they had been called out to.

The firemen have saved many people stranded by water as well as fire. When Eardisley was flooded the fire engine was called upon to bring the children from school through the water to meet the school cars, which were not able to get through the water. The children thought this was a great adventure!

Today's fire service in Eardisley carries on the good work. The fire station is situated just below the church on the opposite side of the main road, and has modern equipment.

Eardisley police officers 1937–2004

The first policeman I remember in Eardisley was PC Edwin Jarrett, who had come to police Eardisley in 1939 and lived in the police house, directly across the road from Mr Powell, in the middle of the village. He was a tall slim man with a moustache and when on duty he was always dressed in his uniform with a tall helmet and a long black cape. He rode a very big bicycle with twenty-eight inch wheels — and he could certainly ride it, as we found out on occasions, as one moment he was here, the next, there. He loved football and told many stories of the times he had played for Herefordshire Constabulary football team, which played Birmingham City Police in 1930. The high spot of his wartime was probably the time when a British light aircraft landed in the Canonford fields. People gathered round in the top corner of the field where the pilot was preparing to take off again, making sure he had enough room to miss the oak trees along the side of the brook, and PC Jarrett directed opera-

As village policeman from 1949 to 1960, PC George Barker (father of my friends Derry and Ron, and pictured here in the lych-gate of Eardisley church) gave me good reason to have a healthy respect for the law throughout my teenage years.

tions. Cape blowing with the airflow from the propeller, he waved his arms to the obedient spectators so as to ensure their safety as the little aircraft bounced across the grass and then gradually lifted above the oak trees, off and away. PC Jarrett was very good to us — I think he kept his eye on us as his grandson Desmond was one of us.

After PC Jarrett retired in 1949 a new house was built for the village policeman along the Kington road. On 2nd March PC George Barker came to live there with his wife, Hilda, and sons, Derry and Ronald, and these two, Derry and Ron, grew up with the rest of us from the time they arrived in Eardisley. The family had come from Wellington, where PC Barker had been the village policeman and greatly respected by the people since 1937. Although Wellington had lost a good man, Eardisley had gained one and PC Barker was very much appreciated for his services in and around Eardisley over the $11^1/_2$ years from 1949 to 1960. He and his family enjoyed Eardisley, joining in with local activities — bell-ringing was one of PC Barker's favourite hobbies — and Eardisley enjoyed them. PC Barker retired in June 1960 and later moved to Madley. Mrs Hilda Barker died on 22nd December 1984 and Mr George Barker died, at the age of 86 years, on 17th February 1991, having been awarded the Queen's Coronation Medal, the Police Long Service Medal and the Defence Medal.

After PC Barker, Eardisley had several police officers, including PC Button, PC Herbert and WPC Lynne Edwards. PC Bill Rowlatt was the last to live in the police house, which has now been sold as a private dwelling. Bill still lives in Eardisley but has retired from the police now and runs his own undertaking business. He has been a great asset to the village, not only in his police work, but also helping with clubs and the church.

Mr Walter Howells

Mr Walter Howells always looked quite serious — he was captain in the Home Guard in the war, but I think that at heart he saw the funny side of things. He was involved a lot with local amateur dramatics, along with people like Jack Moulton, Enid Trumper, Mrs Morris the Folly and my father, Gerald Hales. I think the play I can remember seeing was *The Cuckoo's Nest*. At this time Mr Howell's first wife, Esther, was still alive and they lived in Southway, the wooden bungalow that has only recently been demolished on the corner of the road that now leads down to Forest Fencing. Esther died on 7th April 1963, aged 57 years. Some years later Walter married Peggy Moulton (Norah Nicholas's mother) whose first husband, Jack, had died at the age of 54 on 28th September 1965. Mr Howells tried a lot of different ways of earning a living at various times: he ran the sawmill near Wharf Corner (known as The Electric Sawmill), he built a lot of the houses in the Eardisley area, including (in 1935, the year of King George V's Silver Jubilee) the Jubilee bungalows in Almeley road and our bungalow, and he was an undertaker. He was a business partner of Mr Sidney Jones and with him took over a coal business (though Mr Jones was the one mainly involved in this). He also converted an old building in Winforton into a transport café, The Cross Café. Not only did he renovate this, but, wearing a white apron and with a cloth on his shoulder, he did most of the cooking and serving himself as well. He later sold the café, which became a garage, mainly for Alvis cars, returned to his home in Eardisley and continued his work as a builder and undertaker until he retired. He died on 2nd July 1979 at the age of 90.

Mr Jack Milward

Mr Jack Milward, his wife, Martha, and their family lived in the Eardisley area for a long time and were well known and liked. From when I was very young I

Left, Mrs Mary Milward, Jack's mother, (looking less cheerful than I remember her) with one of her grandchildren, probably in the Thirties. Right, Mr James Milward, Jack's father. I think he died either when I was very young or before I was born.

recall Jack's mother, Mary, coming to my home and talking with my mother. 'Granny' Milward was a lovely lady — warm and caring, a little on the plump side, and always smiling; she reminded me of my own Granny Hales.

Jack was clever in all sorts of ways: he was a good carpenter and his work can be seen in many places locally — he made the two heavy opening gates at the lych-gate and I believe he did some sort of repair or restoration work up in the church bell tower. He could mend things too, and if something couldn't be mended he would make a spare part or improvise. When the Milward family lived at Willersley, us lads would take our motorbike wheels there for Jack to respoke them — Jack would do anything to help if he could. Jack's own motor-cycle back in the Forties and Fifties was a 1927 350 cc Triumph side valve — very old and worn — I remember the fins on the cylinder were rusted and some had dropped off, but he kept it going. For example, when the return spring for the kickstart was broken Jack cut a piece off an old car inner tube to make a

Jack Milward with the new gates he had just made and fitted at the lych-gate, 1976

Jack Milward outside Ideal Bungalow repairing the chain of his Triumph 350 cc motorcycle, early Sixties

strong elastic band and fitted this to the kickstart. It made a perfect return for the job. This was only one of his many improvisations.

As time went on — by now Jack and Martha and the family had moved to Ideal Bungalow at Great Oak — the old Triumph, which had given Jack such good service, began to crack up — after years of running mainly on TVO (tractor vaporizing oil) but having to be started on petrol. (Jack kept a supply of petrol in a Camp Coffee bottle and primed the engine by pouring a small amount into the carburettor; once the engine was going he switched to TVO.) The motorcycle did not run as well on TVO as it would have done on petrol, but that's just the way it was then. Maybe the TVO accounted for its spitting and banging. Looking back to our boyhood days of under-age riding of motorcycles, perhaps it was from Jack that we got the idea of running them on TVO.

Jack's son, George, told me a story from the days when Jack was using the Triumph. One day Jack set off with George riding pillion behind him and his home-made sidecar loaded up with scrap metal to go to the scrap yard. On the way they called in to The Sun at Winforton. After a quick drink they came out again to find that the motorbike and sidecar had gained an admirer — The Law. The police officer asked Jack if he had a 'C' licence but Jack didn't know what he was talking about. The officer explained that if you carry goods you must have a 'C' licence. Jack and George were very bewildered and were given a good talking-to by the officer — all on the subject of the importance of the 'C' Licence — drinking and driving never came into the talk at all!

Jack Milward and his son George with the Triumph 350 cc motorcycle at Willersley in 1955

Jack enjoyed coming down to the pub, mostly with Martha, for a drink and a talk, always leaving home at about 10 pm and returning at 11 pm. There was something magic about those times: the regularity of those journeys, always at 10 o'clock and 11 o'clock, as Jack and Martha made their way down to the village and back home again. Jack would mount his machine and immediately

Jack Milward at Great Oak with his BSA 500 cc motorcycle in 1963

Jack Milward in the early Forties dressed up for some special occasion — he didn't usually look as smart as this!

turn his cap back to front, with the peak facing backwards, so the wind could not blow the cap off — a brilliant idea! (This was fine until crash helmets came in. Jack thought they were dangerous as he found it difficult to hear anything coming from behind.) After kick-starting the bike with Martha sitting on the pillion, Jack would turn it round and head off into the darkness. The bike's lights were not the best but Jack was quite able to cope with the situation as he knew the road well.

In about 1963 Jack decided to get another motorcycle. So he reluctantly parked his faithful Triumph up and bought a 500 cc BSA with a nice sidecar. I am sure this was a proud moment for Jack — although he loved his Triumph this newer bike and sidecar must have been something very special.

Jack died at the age of 69 on 12th October 1981; Martha died on 24th July 2002 aged 81 years.

Chapter Seven: An Impressionable Age

Sam Howells lived in a wooden hut at the sawmill belonging to his nephew, Walter Howells, and Sidney Jones. (This spot is now the workshop of Phoenix Car Restorations.) People spoke of Sam as having once had a wife and family and of problems to do with drink (and I have recently discovered that long ago he had worked at Upper Welson Farm). But when I knew him he had lived alone in the hut for a long time, with just his little dog, Peggy. Peggy was a small spaniel, brown and white — or at least almost white, as she was sometimes a little discoloured from the outside machinery at the sawmill; I think she suffered with a flea problem but she was a good, friendly dog.

Sometimes — when I was about seven or eight — my pal Nick and I would visit Sam in his hut, which was very small — only the size of a garden shed and usually overpoweringly hot as he had a little range-stove in there for cooking. (This seems to me now very dangerous from a fire point of view, especially being on a mill ground with all the timber, but in those days things were different.) Sam seemed very old to us though he was probably still working at the mill at this time. He was short and didn't carry much flesh, very tanned — almost gypsy-looking. I see him in my mind now, with a thick bristly moustache, invariably wearing a trilby hat, probably mixing something up — his meal or whatever — at the table. I can't remember his voice — he didn't speak to us a lot, but I think he enjoyed having our company. We probably stayed there until Mrs Nicholas called Nick for his tea — Sam's hut was just the other side of the fence from their garden. At the time it seemed an exciting thing to pay a visit to Sam: it reminded me of something out of a cowboy film, Sam and his dog, Peggy, in their hut.

Although I didn't see him with them much, I knew Sam had a lot to do with horses and ponies. (Maybe it was partly because of this that he made me think of cowboy films — that and the fact that he looked to me like a slimmer version of Gabby Hayes.) One day I saw him breaking a horse in. I can picture the scene very well — it was in the Barleyclaws field opposite Upper House Farm. Sam looked very determined, lashing out with his whip, and the horse was obviously totally under his control. He had the horse on a lounging rope and kept on tightening it, making him come closer and closer. Eventually he was hitting him on the head with the handle of the whip and drawing blood. This treatment of an animal made a deep and unhappy impression on me: it looked cruel and I hated to see that; I also felt great disappointment that an adult I liked and respected could behave in such a way. If I were to see such treatment of an animal now I would intervene and stop it. I know that this is not how to train a horse to accept a harness or rider. But I think that when it happened I half wondered if this violence was something unavoidable and necessary — something I would understand when I was grown up. And looking back now, although it is horrible to think about, I don't think it is altogether fair to condemn Sam as a cruel man. He was carrying on a tradition and using the horse-breaking methods he had seen used all his life. Thankfully, today we have moved on from this cruel method of breaking horses.

The Baxters were what was known as 'travellers' and my memories of them are from the same sort of time as when Nick and I used to visit Sam Howells. There were five of them, Mr and Mrs Baxter, plus another lady, who I think was the sister of one of them, and two little girls. They lived in an old-fashioned gypsy caravan that could be pulled by a horse — but, as Eardisley was where they mainly lived, the caravan was generally static. It was situated at the bottom of the village where Cam Stables are now, in a corner of a field known as Donkey's Corner. I remember Mrs Baxter — Queenie Baxter — and seeing her

Ellen and Leonard Hales, my father's parents, in the porch of their house at Hobby Lyons four or five years before Grandad died in 1959

driving through the village with a pony and trap. I think Mr Baxter made a living in some sort of way collecting timber but I don't remember him — I have been told that he was a big, rather frightening man and a mate of Sam Howells. Doreen Payne, whose family lived next door, at The Wharf, at that time, said they used to see the two of them set off with the pony and trap to go drinking. When they returned, much the worse for drink, Mr Baxter would bellow: 'Queenie!' at the top of his voice. Mrs Baxter would respond to the summons straightaway, but all she did was look after the piebald brown-and-white pony. She unhitched it from the trap, making the trap tip up, as the weight was at the back end. This caused Mr Baxter and Sam Howells to be unloaded in a most undignified manner. But they were quite used to it. In the meantime, Queenie had returned to the caravan, which was a picture to see — *very* clean and tidy. Doreen says it was beautiful inside (I never saw for myself) but the family never sat down

*'This caused Mr Baxter and Sam Howells to be unloaded
in a most undignified manner.'*

in there — they had their meals outside, sitting round an open fire; when Doreen was playing with the little girls they sat round the fire too. (Doreen remembers her mother being cross with her for getting the smell of smoke on her clothes.) The two girls — one was called Lucy, but Doreen can't remember the other one's name — went to Eardisley school and the family were perfectly well accepted by people in the village, not at all looked down on.

By the time we were about ten we were beginning to look for places where we could earn a bit of pocket money at weekends and after school. The favourite place was the smallholding just out of the village owned and run by Kathleen Darling. Kathleen Adelade Darling — Kitty, as she was known to most people — was the sister of Mr Richard Darling, who had run Modello Works garage and Darling's Buses. Her father had been the doctor in Eardisley, living at Bridge House and having his surgery opposite. He had been a good doctor, well liked, as were all the Darling family.

Kitty was an educated person — I believe she may have had a university degree. When she was a young girl (before my time) she went to Australia. She had lots of clothes and dresses made up by some of the local ladies and off she went, which in those days was a big thing to do. I don't really know what went wrong but she didn't stay long in Australia. She certainly didn't settle and quite soon returned back to Eardisley.

When I knew her she was a short, chubby, middle-aged woman, who seemed to waddle rather than walk. She often wore a khaki, military-style, open-necked shirt with a little cravat-like scarf, a lightweight jacket and trousers, boots or plimsolls, and usually a beret — one of those round ones like the French wear — pulled down, a bit to the right, over unruly hair. She gave the impression she didn't care about herself at all. It was her goats and other people she cared more about. She always seemed to look serious but, deep down, I felt, she had a gentle smile.

She was fond of her goats and looked after them well, knowing each individually — I remember some of their names — Bluebell, Tinkerbell and Daisy. She would bring them in from the fields or orchards to the milking parlour, which was made up especially for them. Each in turn would go up a small ramp onto a platform at the right height for Kitty sitting on a stool. Before milking she always washed the goats' udders and afterwards she made careful records of how much milk each of them had given. When the milk was eventually bottled she would deliver it to her customers using whatever transport she had at the time.

Sometimes she had the goats tethered by chains to stakes in the orchards or fields, so that she could control which areas of grass they ate, and at other times they would be confined in pens made from wooden hurdles that were very strong as they were interwoven. Occasionally the goats had a treat: two local girls about twelve years of age, Joy Prime and Celia Prosser, used to go to Kitty's to do little odd jobs and Kitty would often choose two of the goats to go for a walk with them. The girls and the goats would amble along the lanes together, the girls chattering, the goats wagging their tails and enjoying lush edibles of all sorts away from the competition of the rest of the herd. Now and again Kitty let the goats all run loose for a little while. On one of these occasions I was working there — probably at the bottom of Kitty's garden, which was right next to the orchards. A lady — Miss Busby — had gone to help pick the apples and looking up I saw that one of the goats had noticed Miss Busby bending over invitingly. I could see the goat's mind ticking away: 'What an opportunity!' It looked straight ahead at the target, took a few steps back and then charged! Its

'I could see the goat's mind ticking away: "What an opportunity!"'

horns landed smack on her bum, knocking her to the ground. I can't actually remember what Miss Busby said. She wasn't hurt but she was certainly surprised. As for the goat, it wandered off smugly back to its grazing after the best bit of fun it had had for a long time.

The smallholding consisted of a stone-built house with a couple of fields and orchards, and outbuildings, including a milking parlour for the goats. Approaching the house you went along a narrow stone footpath to get to two high steps up to the front door. This opened directly onto the kitchen/ living room, which I remember as quite something. On the floor there were stone tiles (as there were in all the ground floor rooms); there was a big kitchen table to the left of you as you walked in through the door and an old tea chest to the right of the table. Almost every other bit of floor space was filled with wooden boxes, stacked two-high, used as cupboards and shelves. There was clutter everywhere — tea caddies and tins of all sorts, containing pencils and other bits and pieces, balls of string and binder twine, brushes and combs — probably ones for her and ones for the goats, buckets with cloths for use in the goat-dairy, ripening apples in shallow wooden boxes, bottles of medicine for goats, the odd mug (that probably hadn't seen washing-up water for some time), office paperwork, boxes of matches, working boots or Wellingtons, a candle in a blue enamel holder … and, of course, more stuff for goats.

At the road side of the house, as I remember, (that would be the north), there was a long passage — very narrow, damp and dark; at the end of which was Kitty's pantry. In this passage there were goat skins hanging on the walls, I suppose to cure in some way or other. I never did find out quite what the skins were there for…

As you went through the white six-barred gate across the drive, the strong odours of disinfectant and goat-cleaning fluids and the mellower smells of hay and ripening apples seemed to mix not unpleasantly and linger in the air. I can still recall this smell, which, for me, was unique to Kitty's home. It is a very loveable memory.

Kitty was very inventive. One day we had a job to do in the house which involved going up into the bedroom. After negotiating the stairs and looking around at what we were supposed to do, we noticed something which we thought was unusual: a length of guttering was tied with wire to the handrail going down to the stairs below. Then we saw that at the bottom of the stairs, below the gutter, was a bucket. It was only when we saw another bucket in the bedroom that we put two and two together and wondered if this was how Kitty cracked the problem of going down the garden on dark cold nights … Looking at it from a boy's point of view, I wondered if it was really worth having all this contraption just to avoid carrying a bucket downstairs, but — that was Kitty.

In my earliest memories Kitty drove a horse and trap. She had a lovely horse called Pepper, a little brown mare — Welsh cob type — normally quite a good-tempered animal. I remember one occasion when the horse and trap were tied up to the bus shed at Modello Works. Kitty had been inside the house with my mother and father but had come out again to go home. It was a warm sunny day and there were a lot of flies about — big ones, the sort that used to bite the horses. These flies were annoying Pepper, so Kitty took off her beret and started to swipe at them wildly. Pepper flinched at each swipe and got more and more agitated. It wasn't long before she had had enough bashing with the beret and in pulling and pushing, as she went backwards and forwards, she managed to break loose and take off, trap and all. She careered up through the village towards Kington, the reins dangling precariously close to her hooves and the trap swaying from side to side. Kitty looked surprised and headed off down the yard after Pepper who was now fast disappearing up the road. Seeing this, Kitty's next thought was to find a stick and she came back up the yard looking round for one. Eventually Pepper was caught and brought back to face Kitty and her stick. 'Don't you dare run away again', she muttered to the poor horse — now securely tethered again — who was shying away from the walloping (and probably thinking 'You started it with that ****** beret! Now you're doing the same thing with the stick!'). After giving Pepper this 'lecture' Kitty calmed down. She unfastened the halter, climbed aboard the trap and set off peacefully for home.

Kitty used the horse and trap whenever she came to the village or went to Kington — posting letters, shopping, or whatever. For her an important use was making the deliv-

Bus trip from The Turn, Woodseaves, 1960s.
Left to right, back, Mrs Langford, Mr Langford, Mrs
Hill. Front, Miss Kathleen 'Kitty' Darling, Mrs Page.
For special occasions Kitty sometimes put on a sort of
Panama hat, pulled well down over her eyes.

eries of her goat's milk. This wasn't a milk *round* as you might think; more the odd bottle dropped off now and again, sometimes as late as 8.30 or 9 pm in the summer if she'd forgotten someone earlier in the day. My brother, John, was one of the lucky recipients of Kitty's deliveries (I'm not sure that he actually *liked* the goat's milk but I know he appreciated her kindness). Like a few of her 'customers' he often managed to be out of the way when she arrived with the milk (more than once I heard of someone diving under the table to avoid too long a session with her). He knew that if he was there to take the milk from her he was in for a long conversation — she was never one to hurry when she was talking. I can picture her now, with her eyes closed, thinking exactly what she wanted to say, and then slowly breaking into a little smile as what came to mind struck her as funny. Not so funny for someone cramped under the table, not daring to make the slightest sound, waiting for her to go!

The horse and trap was just the first of many means of conveyance — push-bike, autocycle and eventually motor van — Kitty used over the years for delivering milk and general purposes. Her pushbike was a lady's bicycle with a little cardboard container not much bigger than a shoebox strapped on the carrier at the back. From that she went on to something to help her on the hills and she bought an autocycle. Later she decided to learn to drive. This was fine until the day when she misjudged the corner whilst taking her Austin 7 van towards Woodseaves and ended up driving an amphibious vehicle through the deep pond that used to be beside the highway — quite a shock to the ducks as well as Kitty!

After running into the pond Kitty decided to pack up driving, but in later years she took it up again. By this time the Austin 7 was quite old but it still served its purpose. It was small and basically square — as Austin 7s were — built with fabric around a wooden structure. It had a very small return on the clutch pedal, and would sometimes get oil on the clutch plate, so that it would have been difficult for anyone to drive smoothly — let alone Kitty — but with Kitty at the wheel it leaped up and down alarmingly — it was hilarious to watch. On one occasion, coming down from the Almeley road to the village, Kitty stopped at the junction by The New Inn and looked left and right. She pulled away jerkily and went into a series of bounds as if the van were running on kangaroo fuel — the poor goats must have been thrown up and down and sideways as the van made its way across the main road to the Woodseaves road.

Once, while driving with three or four goats in the back, Kitty discovered how much stronger stone was than fabric and wood. Hobby Lyons bridge has always been quite hard to negotiate — and it was especially so for her — what with the need to go up and over and steer round an acute narrow bend (flanked by stone pillars and metal railings) at the same time. On this particular occasion she caught one of the pillars at the side of the bridge. This opened up a big hole in the side of the van. At first the goats were bewildered. But as soon as they came to their senses they saw daylight through the hole in the van and then, without further hesitation, made for open air and freedom. I'm not sure how Kitty got them home after that, but I wouldn't be at all surprised if she didn't end up fixing chains to their collars and leading them home on foot.

The last of these mishaps came on the day when, returning home to The Field, Kitty misjudged the steering on the steep ramp up into her garage. The front wheel went over the edge and the whole van tipped over and fell two or three feet down onto its side. After this, the little van's days (with Kitty anyhow) were finished and, for Kitty, it was back to pedal power.

Kitty's barns and other loft areas were usually full of hay that had been cut and made by some of us and then brought from the fields to the barns with the BMB Garden Tractor. This was a two-wheeled tractor with a two-wheeled bogey behind it. The driver sat on the bogey controlling the tractor — at least that was the idea but it was quite an achievement to do this. It had a 6-hp Jap engine (quite powerful for the size of the machine). To start it you had to wrap a belt round a pulley and then give a swift tug. Sometimes it started straightaway but on other occasions, if you didn't pull it over with confidence, it might fire in the wrong direction, pulling you with it. All the controls were on the long steering handlebars, so any kind of manoeuvring — steering round an obstacle, negotiating a slope up or down, trying to stop even — had to be done from a position with arms stretched out far in front of the bogey and wide apart — difficult and awkward for anyone and particularly so for a young lad without adult strength. The whole thing could be a bit of a rat-trap if one of the wheels caught on something, and when you wanted to stop you could find yourself halfway up an old tree stump or in a ditch.

But many good times and laughs were had by everyone who had the plea-sure of driving her. I think it was Humphrey Plumstead who held the speed record, as on one occasion while he was going down the lane to the hay field he lost control and jumped off, leaving the tractor and trailer to their own devices in the brook at the bottom of the hill — at least they got washed. The little trailer didn't carry much hay — I think we might have been quicker with a wheelbarrow — but that's the way it was.

Kitty took down the hours we worked in a book as we went along and worked out the pay. Then on pay-day she sat behind the pay-desk (the tea chest in the kitchen) and we stood in front while she paid us. Mostly we would use the money for little perks such as going to the pictures or maybe buying some-thing for our home-made-up bikes, such as a puncture outfit or a mudguard. Whatever it was we were pleased to get it. Harvest time was a good time to be working for Kitty, lots of fun, and pay was top rate for us then — probably about a shilling or two. We would then come out of the house and down the steps to the garden path smiling and very pleased with ourselves: 'Look out Hereford!' Sometimes we would earn enough money to go to the pictures or the swim-

Mrs Annie Page, possibly in the early Fifties. We often saw Mrs Page about the village on her 3-wheeler. She was a cheerful, good-natured person, who I think had originally come from Ireland. She and Mr Page lived in a cottage at Lower Welson.

ming baths, *then* have a meal of fish and chips, and *then* come back by train! (It always seemed better to go and come back by train, more fun somehow.) Kitty kept going a long time with only the help she received from youngsters in the village, but in later years I think she had more regular help from a chap called Bill Milward.

I must not stay too long writing of Kitty but there are so many stories about her — stories about her smallholding, her animals, her vehicles and her machines — but I'll finish with just mentioning her regular late arrival at church. The service would be well underway — probably fifteen or twenty minutes would be gone by — and then, in the quiet of the service, the large church door would clonk. Most of the congregation would try not to take any notice knowing that as usual it was just Kitty being late.

With all her daftness and the antics she got up to, she was a very genuine, nice, kind person. I don't think it was until much later in life that I realized just what a 'tidy' person she was. And I think a lot of people are like me in this: at the time we just thought she was funny, but now she's gone (Kitty died on 6th April 1966) we miss her.

Mr Page with the 3-wheeler cycle he and Mrs Page both used — which we had such fun with on a few occasions when it was parked at Modello Works — late Forties perhaps

Eardisley and the parishes around it have been fortunate over the years in their parsons — people such as the Rev. W Reginald Griffiths, who came to Eardisley in the late Forties when I was about twelve, after the Rev. Sydney Osborne. He was a thick set man, not very tall — what I would call a 'tidy' person — always a pleasure to talk to in his quiet way. He was a big lift to the village and parish, particularly taking an interest in activities for young people, setting up youth clubs, scouts and cadets, amongst other things. My pals and I were involved with him in many of these and found him an excellent man, a real leader. We all respected him

The Rev. W R Griffiths, rector of Eardisley 1949–1959. This photo shows him in his study in Brilley in about 1960, shortly after he had left Eardisley.

Ladies from Eardisley British Legion at a tea party at Brilley rectory given by the Rev. Reg Griffiths about 1959.
Left to right, back, Mrs Dick Darling (May), Mrs Oliver Jones (Rose), Mrs Lewis Vallender (Nancy), Mrs Jack Moulton (Peggy) — later Mrs Walter Howells, Mrs Trevor Turner (Brenda), Mrs Charlie Nicholas (Freda), Mrs James (Bessie), Mrs Hubert Williams (from Whitney), Miss Gertrude Trumper, Miss Lilian Gwatkin, Mrs Page (Alice), Miss Lil Trumper.
Front, Miss Ethel Southgate, Miss Gertrude Brookes, Miss Annie Smith, Mrs Page (Annie), Mrs Reg Griffiths (Mary), Miss Doris Jones, Mrs Tong, Mrs Douglas Jones (Edith), Mrs Philpotts (Bertha), Mrs Tippins (Alice)

and learned a lot from him. In 1958 Rev. Griffiths moved from Eardisley to Brilley and we missed him very much, although Eardisley was again fortunate in having a good man to take over the parish, the Rev. Frank Willford, who came in March 1959.

The Eardisley army cadets corps was formed in about 1949 and run by Mr Glyn Jones (Nesta Stephens's father), with Rev. Griffiths as the cadet parson. When cadets first started, sessions took place in a Nissen hut at the former American camp. The unit was well supported and, as well as learning to be soldiers — by learning map reading and shooting, and by going on night manoeuvres and other activities — we had a lot of good times. Later a hut was built specially on the other side of road, near what is now the barn conversions, about 100 yards to the left of the pound. I joined the cadets at a very early age. (It is funny how one's age jumps when one wants to be able to join something.) After some time in the cadets and a fortnight at Penally army camp in Wales, however, I began to change my mind. I thought that the very early swims in the cold sea, the long marches (as they seemed to be) and the early morning bugle waking you up to a mess tin of porridge or something equivalent, were not for me. After about a year I left the cadets and joined the scouts with the rest of my pals. (Later on, the cadet hut became a hut for the scouts.)

Army cadets at Penally camp near Tenby about 1949.
Left to right, back, Peter Hill and another boy (both from Kington), Robert Knights, Derry Barker.
Front, a boy from Kington and me

Mr Glyn Jones, who ran cadets, had an electrical business in Eardisley and was one of the first people in the village to do much with TV. He also charged accumulators and delivered them around to his customers. Usually this was done by Derry Barker who was working for Glyn as a lad for £1 a week. This was in 1949. Derry wanted to learn the electrical trade and so he was willing to go round fitting TV aerials with Glyn. Mr Glyn Jones was also a disc jockey — one of the first people I remember doing this. He had his records at different functions — dances and parties — and his public address system at local sports and shows.

Someone else who helped with scouts was Mr Rowland Webb, who lived at The Institute with his wife and was caretaker of the village hall for many years. He was well known in the village as he always did a lot of work behind the scenes. Mr Webb was a great help and always made himself useful, preparing meals, cleaning up and generally looking after the welfare of the lads.

I went to scout camp with my friends on several occasions. I remember when we camped as a scout group in Borth on the side of the hill by the sea front. The Rev. Griffiths was with us, as was Mr Webb. After pitching our camp and settling down for a meal which the two had prepared for us, we, or *some* of us I should say, got to sleep. But not for long because it started to rain very heavily and then turned into a nasty storm with the water running through the tents. Most of us got out and started to dig trenches around the tents, which we should

Scout camp at Borth, about 1952.
Left to right, me, Tony Goodwin, Elwyn

have done before the storm. Everyone got rather wet that night (except for one or two who slept through it all) but it didn't really matter as it seemed to be quite an adventure for us. At least we soon dried out and enjoyed the rest of the week.

Another camp I remember was the one at Roose in Cumbria. It was very hot and we were all sunbathing, lying in the hot sun, having a sleep in the fields above our camp. The sun was beating down and beginning to burn our bodies and I noticed a short thickset man slowly and quietly passing by but saying nothing. When I realized what was happening it was Mr Griffiths checking that the lads were all right, and gently putting towels

Eardisley Tennis Club, probably about 1950.
Left to right, back row, unidentified lady, Miss Madeline Powell, Miss Olive Davies (now Morgan), John Fellowes, Ernie Crump, Bill Murrell, Bill Davies (from The Castle, Olive's grandfather), Mrs Joan Povey (née Morrison). Middle row, Mrs Edith Morris (née Foley), Miss Freda Pritchard, the Rev. Reginald Griffiths. Front row, Isabel Smith, Edna Smith, Muriel Parry, Mrs Isobel Bateson, Mrs Mary Griffiths.
Some of us lads from the village would often volunteer to mow the grass on the tennis courts — we enjoyed it really as the mower was driven by an engine!
For cutting the grass we would get the occasional game but we were quite happy just to watch the others play.

over the shoulders of the vulnerable ones so that they did not get burnt by the sun. That was the sort of man he was. How fortunate we were to have men like Mr Webb and the Rev. Griffiths to take us on such wonderful camps

In 1959 the Rev. Griffiths moved on from Eardisley and he eventually ended up in The Garth in Kington, where he died. Mr Rowland Webb died on 13th October 1957. Although both these men are dead, the memories of them will stay with me and I am sure many other people will remember them too.

Frank Moulton was an Eardisley lad who I grew up with until 1953, when he joined the navy, as a boy entrant, at the age of 15. At that time he was living with his parents, Peggy and Jack Moulton, and brother and sister, Stuart and Norah, at the post office. One winter day, while Frank was home on leave from the navy not long after he had joined, without his father's permission he decided to take his 4/10 shotgun across the fields at the back of his house to shoot a rabbit or two. After a while, having no luck, he turned back to come home empty-handed, but he slipped in the snow and the gun, which he had not broken, went off, shooting Frank in the leg. He fell to the ground, bleeding badly and, unable to move, shouted for help.

Luckily, some distance away there were local youngsters sledging in the snow, Prue Plumstead, John Carter and Donald Steptoe. At first they took little notice of the shouting, but eventually they went to see what it was all about and discovered Frank in a bad way. Prue, who was only nine or ten at the time, says 'There was blood and gore everywhere'. They went for help and Frank's father came out from the post office, together with Miss Edith Brown, who was then living at East View (now known as The Dairy House). Edith and Mr Moulton quickly took a gate off its hinges and used it as a stretcher to carry Frank home. When Dr Smythe came he ripped open Frank's trousers with a knife, revealing a terrible wound. Frank was taken to hospital in Hereford and treated in one of the hut buildings — where it is said that he got frostbite in his toes! He remained in hospital for some weeks and took a long time to make a full recovery but, like many others, I believe it is partly because of the quick action of Prue, John and Donald that Frank has since been able to live a normal life.

While he was convalescing at home Frank began to feel left out: he wanted to join in with the rest of us lads in the village. Then he had an idea: he would see if he could borrow the basket wheelchair from the rectory and get us to 'tush' him round. Rev. Griffiths lent Frank the chair very willingly. It had two

'Frank shot past, the chair's braking system (if there was one) being very poor.'

106

large wheels with solid tyres at the back and a small wheel at the front. The small wheel was connected by a long bar to a crosspiece at the end, so that the person sitting in the chair could steer (or attempt to — sometimes the contraption seemed to have a mind of its own). There was a bar behind the seat for someone to push the chair but it wasn't long before we were taking turns to tow Frank in the Bath chair behind our bikes as we rode around Kinnersley, Almeley and elsewhere. We used quite an amount of binder twine, as it broke now and again when we stopped and Frank shot past, the chair's braking system (if there was one) being very poor. I think going downhill was the worst. I do not recall what we did in those circumstances — probably just had an anchor man hooked to the back of the chair. But Frank survived and seemed happy just to be with us.

Group, including members of the Davies family from Castle Farm and the Layton family from Parton Farm, outside the Methodist chapel about 1952.
Left to right, back row, Noreena Nash, Marian Jones, John Charles, Desmond Jarrett — grandson of PC Jarrett, unknown man, Gordon Holmes, Peggy Layton, Graham Jones — son of Sid Jones, the coal merchant, Jeanette Layton, Mrs Marian Triffitt. Second row, Richard Carter — son of the Carters who for some time ran the shop at Arboyne House, Mrs Edith Tomlinson, unknown girl, Olive Davies, Brenda Layton, Jill Davies, Clive Davies.
Third row, unknown girl, Thelma Morgan, Megan Charles, Anne Charles. Nesta Jones, Anne Jones, sister of Graham Jones, John Carter — brother of Richard Carter. Front row, unknown boy, Tony Jenkins, Prunella Plumstead, Betty Vallender, Olwen Layton, Myra Davies, Ken Charles

He did not rejoin the navy. For a while after he was back on his feet he worked as a porter in a hospital in St Albans and some years later, when he was fully recovered from his injuries, he joined the army — the Royal Signals — and eventually made it his career. He is now retired.

Chapter Eight: Men Being Boys

After coming out of The New Inn one night, and feeling a little jovial, a few of the locals — James Morris, Peter Preece, David Morgan and David Powell — got talking and were just about to make for home when James asked Peter if he had a ladder handy. Peter said yes, and went and fetched the ladder, wondering what James had in mind. He soon found out. In the garden just across the road from The New Inn, at Arboyne House, where Mr Bruce Povey lived, was a fir tree. James rested the ladder against this tree, climbed up and fixed a fused crow-scarer to it. (Crow-scarers are used by farmers for scaring birds off crops. They are a bit like a firework about the size of a pencil, and when you light one it goes off with a noise like gunshot.)

James Morris. The first time I remember James was when he was dressed up to be the prisoner for the Home Guard exercise.

The chaps then made their way down the village to the yew tree on the Doctor's bridge and fixed a crow-scarer there. They repeated the procedure on a tree by the post office and again on the telegraph pole opposite Mr Brierley's butcher's shop, linking them all together like fairy lights with a long fuse. At about 11 o'clock they went back and lit the fuse. Then they went home and waited for the outcome.

Soon there was a loud bang … and a few minutes later another … and then another. People looked out of their bedroom windows in their night clothes to see what the noise was all about.

'I can see you!' someone called out bravely. But of course he couldn't see the culprits as they had gone a long time ago.

Mr Brierley realized what was causing the commotion when he spotted a red glow across from his house, and he went down into the street to put an end to it. Mr Jack Brookes also came out to investigate, caught sight of someone behaving suspiciously and started giving him stick. Mr Brookes then discovered that the suspicious stranger was actually Mr Brierley and was full of apologies. Eventually everyone went back to bed — though by this time there wasn't much time left for sleep as morning was coming round fast.

Elwyn Nicholas was always fun to have around. On the day of the sports and carnival one year, before going along to the field, Elwyn dropped in for a pint at The New Inn. When he came out of the pub he saw that not much traffic was forking left off the main road at The Tram to drive in the direction of the sports field, so he decided to do something about it. Taking up an 'official' position in the middle of the road, he proceeded to direct all cars up towards Sheepcroft field. This caused considerable confusion as a lot of the drivers were *not* on their way to the sports, and most turned round and came back down to the village looking quite bewildered. Fortunately for public order, a sharp-eyed policeman cottoned on to what Elwyn was doing and had a word with him. But everything was taken in good spirit and the show was a success.

He was quite one for dressing up and playing the fool. I remember one time — probably in the late Sixties or early Seventies — when he and David Powell went to a fancy dress barn dance that was being held in a big barn belonging to Mr and Mrs Ken Davies at Yew Tree Farm in Kinley, which is just west of Letton. David was dressed up as a baby in just a nappy (made from a bath towel) secured with a large safety pin, and a huge dummy. Elwyn was the mother, very smart in a long green dress and feather boa, a wig and hat, and high-heeled shoes. Leaving Elwyn's house, where they had put on their costumes, Elwyn saw a football on the path. Forgetting that he was wearing a long tight skirt he gave it a hefty kick — and promptly went flying. He picked himself up and they left for The New Inn, to collect the pram and load the baby into it. It was a

'All of a sudden there was a crash as the pram hit a concrete step and the poor baby was catapulted out.'

Nick and Norah (née Moulton) Nicholas — perhaps before they were married

nice solid old-fashioned sprung pram — a Silver Cross one that had done service for lots of babies in David's family. Unfortunately it wasn't made for a baby the size of this one and as they began to go into the pub it collapsed, throwing out the baby. At this point they hadn't even got to the barn dance and the parade! They spent some time drinking in The New Inn, Elwyn joking as he always did and getting in the mood. David in his attire was, not surprisingly, a bit of a target for a few of the locals who could not resist the opportunity to use the pot of mustard at the bar to make the baby's nappy a little more realistic. David did not budge and took it all in his stride. Then off they went to the barn. When they got there they hastily patched up the pram and then the strapping baby climbed into it again. Then the mother began to push the pram round the barn. Round and round 'she' went with great energy, playing up enthusiastically to the wolf whistles of the spectators and scarcely looking where 'she' was going. All of a sudden there was a crash

Nick, left, and Keith Needes in the 1950s

Nick aged about 15 or 16

as the pram hit a concrete step and the poor baby was catapulted out. David hit his head on something very hard and was momentarily knocked out. But as soon as he came round, he got back into the pram. Elwyn adjusted his dress and the evening's entertainment carried on.

Another of the Eardisley characters was Mr Dave Harvey, who lived in the village for some years and, soon after the previous landlord, Mr Reg Jones, died, became the landlord of The New Inn in 1972, renaming it The Mountie.

Dave did a lot for the village, putting time and effort into many activities, but he is particularly remembered for functions such as the British Legion's stampedes and the Hedgehog Hunt. The first stampede, in 1971, was held just out of the village in a field off the Almeley road, opposite the cricket field. There were competitions of all sorts, but the main attraction was riding the

Taking the plunge at (a very muddy) Eardisley Stampede in Kinnersley, 1st June 1979

bullocks — it was more like being in the Wild West than a Herefordshire village. The stampede had been well advertised and a huge crowd came from all over. At first, the vehicles arriving at the field queued to be admitted, but, as time went on, the people on the gates just had to let them in as best they could — the queue stretched across the field and right down to the main road and was causing a traffic jam. All the visitors really enjoyed themselves and, largely on account of Dave's organizing ability, the stampede was a big success.

The Hedgehog Hunt, like so many other things that make Eardisley interesting, was arranged in one of the two pubs — in this case The Mountie. (As one person who remembers it well says, 'It was just an excuse for a drink!') Posters were put up, at The Mountie and in a different Kington pub each week, announcing the next hedgehog hunt. But all that happened was that ten or so people, including Dave with his dog Rommel, would leave The Mountie for Kington and spend half the night drinking. No hedgehog hunting ever took place!

Somehow, round about 1974, ITV came to hear about the Hedgehog Hunt, and sent John Swallow to film it, but, as it was supposed to take place at night, no filming was done because the film crew were only here for a short time in the afternoon. Later, the BBC sent St John Howell to film the hunt for the *Midlands Today* programme. The BBC crew also arrived in the afternoon and they spent some time 'setting the scene' in the village. St John Howell, speaking to camera, said the most exciting thing to take place generally in Eardisley was an occasional whist drive. At this Mrs Arthur Prosser rushed out of her garden at Cartref, next to The Tram, to put him straight! He eventually got away half an hour later.

Filming started at The Mountie at about 6 pm. The opening shots were supposed to be of drinking-up time: Jack Milward (who in reality always drank at The Tram and not until 10 pm) was to be filmed drinking up after Dave had called 'Time'. Jack turned up at The Mountie at 5.45 and began drinking. By the time the scene was properly set and the cameras were rolling Jack certainly had 'drunk up' — six pints, at the BBC's expense! At 8 o'clock the crew went up into the fields to film a few local characters togged out in wellies and coats, plus Dave Harvey's dog, which he claimed was bred specially for the job, with a bit of hedgehog-like grunting coming from a couple of chaps hidden behind a hedge. In the middle of all this PC Rowlatt turned up to see what the lights and noise were about. It is alleged he was told 'B****r off! We're BBC'. At 10.30 they all returned for some more drinking and then, at nearly midnight, they decided to film Roy King being woken from his sleep by a phone call from Dave saying hedgehogs had been sighted. (This was done at Roy's mother's house at 9 Canonford Avenue because she had a telephone. Mrs Davies's house next door was also floodlit, which did not please her at all, and she slammed her door shut in St John Howell's face.) Roy was shown getting ready for the night's hunt and setting off to meet the other hunters at The Mountie, where he had a little refreshment before they all went down the steps and out into the night. As usual the order of filming was quite different from the order in which the actual events would have happened (if they really had!).

The feature lasted about five minutes on the *Midlands Today* programme and that was more or less the end of the Eardisley Hedgehog Hunt.

No hedgehogs were ever actually involved in the hedgehog hunts, but an animal that really did play a part in the village's life was Peppi, the pet donkey at The Tram Inn in the 1970s, owned by the then landlord and lady, Mr and Mrs Leonard Lewis. Peppi was a great attraction for the customers. He was often seen having a drink at the bar or chewing a cigarette or two, and getting up to all sorts of antics, from having a dance with the landlord to joining in the festive activities, and he sometimes had to be turned out.

On a cold winter's day Peppi would look bedraggled, the longish hair of his coat wet from the rain and beginning to freeze. But he was clever; he had learnt a way of overcoming the wet and cold. He watched the lounge door and if it was left open a moment he was there, icicles and all, and then he went straight to the fireplace and lay down on a cosy mat in front of a blazing wood fire, ignoring everyone, until he had dried out. Once dry and warm, if he didn't go

Peppi the donkey, with Jill and Leonard Lewis, in the bar of The Tram, 1970s

to sleep he sometimes wandered round the room, perhaps having a drink or a chew at the cigarettes in the ashtrays. If he was unable to get into the lounge he had a back-up shelter — the outside toilets. Here he sometimes stayed if it was raining, looking out through the door miserably until he was able to seize the opportunity to make for the lounge, where he got spoiled by the customers. This cheered him up and he was soon back to fun and games.

'Time' came for Peppi when Len and Jill Lewis finished at The Tram Inn and Peppi had to move on. But as far as I know he is living happily somewhere in the Builth Wells area. We all wish him well — what a character!

Returning to the human characters — there were two Jim Morgans in the village. One was actually called Cyril, and was Wilf Morgan's brother. He worked hard on local farms most of his life, apart from the time when he was in the Forces — as soon as they started looking for volunteers, Cyril put down his pikel and went straight to sign up. This must have been a great loss to Percy Powell, who farmed at Welshwood where Cyril was helping at the time, as he was a good workman. Over the years Jim would often take part in local events such as the sports and carnival. He had little party pieces — reciting 'The Green Eye of the Little Yellow God' and singing Jim Reeves numbers — which he did looking very smart in a black bow tie. Sometimes, at parties in his own home, Knapp House, he would jump up on a pig bench, using it as an improvised stage. The sporting side for James usually took place outside the beer tent, joking with the locals. Taking part in the carnival one year James dressed up as a parson; with his collar and gown he decided to do his rounds in the village as the new parson for Eardisley and went on his rounds talking to people and introducing himself. After a lot of drinks of different sorts he returned to the tent where his flock welcomed him with a cheer. He would do anything to make a smile and was popular among all who knew him.

The 'real' Jim Morgan used to live at Northway, a little way up the road from the Methodist chapel. He had been a paratrooper in the last war and was very proud of the fact. When he came home from the war he worked as an electrician and eventually got his own business going in Eardisley. Jim was well known and popular with people around the area for the things he got up to — such as putting things in someone else's basket in a supermarket when they weren't looking and then waiting to observe the outcome (usually a puzzled argument between a husband and wife). Often Kath Harvey was with him on these outings and she remembers a time when it was four cans of beer he craftily slipped into a trolley. What Jim didn't realize was that while he was doing that, Kath was being just as crafty and slipping a haggis into *his* trolley — and he was so busy laughing about the beer that he didn't notice the haggis amongst his shopping until he unpacked it at home!

He would often be dressed up in the local carnival. By this stage in his life he was quite a portly figure and he usually chose a character that fitted his appearance. One time, I remember, he dressed up as Churchill. On another occasion I can vividly picture him dressed up as Norman Schwarzkopf — 'Storming Norman'. Standing in an original American open Jeep in combat style, with his son-in-law Philip Radziejowski driving, Jim was making a professional salute from a proud military stance as they drove off from Tram Square.

The last time I ever saw him was in 1995 when it was Christmas Eve. I was in The Tram and he came up to me and asked if I had my Father Christmas outfit with me (as I often took it there at Christmastime). I did and he put it on straightaway and started to sing at the top of his voice 'How great Thou art'. This gave a great lift to the evening: people started to sing along with him, making a very special atmosphere. As the evening came to a close, Jim and I left the bar to go home. As we got outside Jim turned to me and said, 'Bri, look up there above the door.' I looked and saw that Jim had fixed above the door what appeared to be a pair of passion-killers wishing everyone a Merry Christmas. I smiled and then, as we walked on towards home, he explained that *he* had put them there — and why. Two years ago Mr Alan Hall, an occasional drinking companion of his who had lived for a while in Arboyne House, had asked Jim if he would hang this garment up at The Tram one Christmas. At the time Alan asked this he was very ill — he would have done it himself otherwise — and not long afterwards he

Jim Morgan as 'Storming' Norman Schwarzkopf at one of Eardisley's carnivals on the Sheepcroft field — in about 1990. His son-in-law, Philip Radziejowski, is driving, and two of the three grandsons who were there in the back of the Jeep, Stewart Probert, Jim Lewis and Michael Larke, can be seen in this picture. On the right, just visible, with a young rider sitting with him on his horse Beauty, is Alexander McLeod-Black. Alexander lived in Eardisley for eleven years from 1987, and usually assumed the role of a cowboy — Tex the Cowboy. Here he seems to playing the part of Big Chief Tex the Injun for a change!

died. Jim showed me that he'd done what Alan had asked and seemed pleased that he had fulfilled Alan's request.

Arriving outside his house — Northway — Jim invited me in for coffee. I hesitated as by now it was gone midnight, and I really was tired. But as Margaret was on night duty and Jim lived alone — his wife Eileen had died some years earlier — and by now it was actually Christmas

Jim Morgan's famous horned rabbit, as exhibited at several Eardisley village festivals, 1990s

morning, I decided to go in for short time to keep him company. After nattering for a bit over a cup of coffee we heard a knock on the door. When Jim opened the door Jossy Bounds and her sister Caroline were there. They'd seen Jim's light on as they walked home and decided to call in to have an early Christmas drink. Because they'd arrived and Jim had now got company I decided

Jim Morgan in the 1990s with an example from his taxidermy collection in a case behind him

to say goodnight and go home, which I did. Next morning, around 11 o'clock, a knock came on my door and there was Caroline. 'Brian', she said, 'I can't believe it. Jim's died.' I couldn't believe it myself and so I went down and found his neighbour, Philip Wilson, who told me Jim had died after getting all ready to go out to his daughter's for Christmas lunch: he had dressed up in his Sunday best and fed the dogs, and he must just have died as he waited to be collected by his family. He was 71 years old.

Chapter Nine: Changes

Eardisley village experienced a very bad flood through the main street in about 1959. It was evening time, down came the rains and it was not long before the drains became blocked and the brooks overflowed. The water got so deep that it washed an Austin 7 car from High Gardens (by The Tram Inn) down the village to the metal railing beside Modello Garage. After that another car, a Morris, was washed from the Reading Room by the village hall. It finished up

1959 floods in Eardisley. This Austin 7, belonging to Reg Weale, was washed down the village from High Gardens (opposite the Methodist chapel). It was swept in and out of driveways and eventually came to rest against another car, a Morris Oxford belonging to Jack Davies. The Morris had been parked by the village hall, had floated past Modello Works and stopped eventually against the railings at Modello. The old Eardisley fire station can just be seen in the background, with the fire siren on the tall metal post between the fir tree and the telegraph pole. This picture was taken from just outside Brook House (where Jean Sharples lives now) looking towards Modello Works — the look of things here was much more open then than it is now. The stanks were just behind the left-hand side of the car and my father used to go there to test tubes for punctures in the water.

The flood in 1959 outside Brook Farm. (The houses just to the right of the telegraph pole are the Wilkin cottages.) The brook here is normally six or seven feet from the road so at the time this photo was taken the water level of the brook had risen five or six feet.

The flood in 1959 outside Brook Farm. This picture shows the situation a little later when the water has receded a bit.

parked next to the Austin. At the bottom of the village I had been doing a job for a local farmer as the storm broke out. After a while he said, 'I had better run you home in the Land Rover', which he tried to do, but we could only get as far as the Doctor's bridge, just below my home.

After helping a neighbour of mine just south the bridge, I decided to try and get home to Ashcroft, which was not many yards away but difficult to reach because of all the water. I managed to get onto the railings, which the two cars had come to rest on, and crawled across the roofs of the cars — by then the water was going in through the driver's windows. I then managed to crawl across some more railings into the yard of my home where I was shocked to find my mother and father mopping up our bungalow. Most of the houses, garages and shops in the top part of the village were flooded, but I had never before known floods to reach high enough to get into the bungalow.

The 1959 flood at The Field. The people in the picture (the Langfords) are looking at an enormous tree, which fell down into the brook after the floodwater had washed the earth from its roots. The car in the picture is a very old Austin 7 belonging to Jack Langford but it originally belonged to Mr Barker the village policeman. I remember two other things about this place. One was that to get to The Drails, where we used to pick wild daffodils, you used to go through a gate about 20 yards to the right of the shed on the right of this picture. The other was that there used to be huge numbers of pigeons here — the Langfords liked and fed them and the birds roosted on the roofs of the house and outbuildings. Not long after old Mr Langford died the pigeons flew away and never returned.

Tram Inn flood 1959. The man in the middle is the landlord at The Tram, Gordon Parker; the others are various locals. The trailer had probably been lent by a farmer to collect debris from the flood.

Both the pubs were flooded but this didn't stop the drinking — especially by those with wellingtons — though one man was supposed to have swum from The New Inn to The Tram Inn in an earlier Eardisley flood, but I think maybe it was more like an overarm crawl with the occasional foot off the ground. (I think he then waited for 'low tide' before returning to The New Inn.)

A certain gentleman who I think you will know — with one arm and always immaculate — was among those drinking at The New Inn. He was looking through the window at the water rushing by and laughing with the other customers at what they saw — logs, branches and all sorts of bits of timber. It was quite a joke when they realized that some of these pieces of wood were from an outside toilet. This gentleman was less amused when he eventually arrived home to find that it had been *his* privy that had been floating past the pub.

When I was a child, the brook was open from Modello Works to where it went under the Doctor's bridge, and there were wooden sluice gates (which we called *stanks*) controlling the flow of water. The bridge itself had quite a hump and vehicles sometimes left the ground if they went over the bridge at speed — as a few characters did for fun. This area was a great place for children to play: paddling in the

MEB Hillman van at Gypsy Hall bridge, Almeley Road, in the 1959 flood. I think the driver must have assumed there was just a little water across the road and that he would be able to drive through. But he must very soon have realized that the bridge had been completely washed away, leaving a deep void where it had been.

The High St looking south. You can still see the yew tree that used to be on the bridge in this picture.

stream in wellingtons, catching fish with nets and bent pins and crouching under the bridge as the traffic went overhead.

But there was not so much traffic then. Also, the village used to flood quite badly. Today things have been improved a lot. Sometime in the 1960s the brook was piped and covered over. As the main road through the village has been resurfaced the road has progressively been raised higher, taking a lot of the hump off the bridge and leaving the high-fliers grounded. A huge, very old, yew tree, which was half in Jean Sharples' garden and half on the pavement, was cut down on 6th July 1981 to make more room for traffic and a pavement. And the bridge itself, which was built for the horses and carriages of years ago, has been strengthened to take today's traffic. Still, it's sad when you think of the fun the children used to have there.

In 1971, my brother John and my brother-in-law (Shirley's husband) Norman Allan, as J W Hales and Company, bought the business from my father and Ernie Crump. John and Norman at first ran the garage as a repair workshop for plant-hire machines and equipment, employing a lot of local labour, and then for a short time extended into selling Land Rovers, at that time in big demand. For a while I worked for J W Hales & Co myself, before going on to run my own small contracting business for about sixteen years. I enjoyed this, and met a lot of wonderful people. It is good to see the work one has done all over the place. Eventually, in 1976, shortly after John and Norman had agreed to go their separate ways, they sold Modello Works. (John briefly ran a plant-hire business on his own from Modello, but then moved to Woonton and spent some years in market gardening.) Most of my family have been in some sort of business or another, from Benny Higgs, my grandad in Abersychan, who ran a greengrocery, and my father, brother and brother-in-law, to Brenda, my daughter, who is in partnership with an estate agent in The Forest of Dean.

The new owners of Modello Works — Franklin and Hodge — used the premises as a workshop for metal fabrication. This business was successful but in due course it moved elsewhere and Mr Franklin and Mr Hodge parted. Peter Hodge remained in Eardisley and, for a year or two (round about 1980), he let out Modello Works as a recording studio. After that it was sold and used for a while as a greengrocery. Finally, in the late Eighties, it was sold again and turned into a house, three storeys high, with beautiful beams — a picture to see.

When the building became a house its name was changed from Modello Works to The Malt House (as that was what we

My parents above Llangwnnadl beach, September 1972. Not long after this picture was taken, in 1974, my mother died, aged 66 years. Two years later, at the age of 68, my father died.

think it once used to be). This transformation to house from garage was mainly carried out by Mr Allen Wilding, who now lives in the village, as did his father, Mr Leslie Wilding, who I knew for many years. Mr Peter Preece bought The Malt House and let it out for a while — before selling it back to Allen Wilding. Allen had by now established a carpet-making business and the long bus shed at the back was ideal for housing his looms. Allen did some more work on the house and the surrounding buildings and then sold the front part, now called March House. March House has so far had a couple of owners. These people have seemed happy to be there, which is not surprising as it really is a lovely building. I never thought I would see Modello Works so completely transformed. I often wonder what my father and Mr Crump would make of it all.

My friend Brian Jones, who I still think of as Nowt, has had a very interesting life — much more than I can write about.

After returning from National Service in the army, Brian was still looking for adventure, and he decided to join an overland travel firm just starting up in Hereford called Penn Overland Tours. He joined them as a driver mechanic and his first job was to get a BMC bus ready for a trip to India. Then, in December 1959, he set off on the tour as driver, encountering all sorts of

Children from Eardisley school in 1961 outside Southway, the wooden bungalow that was on the corner of Church Road and Orchard Close until it was demolished in 2004. Mr and Mrs Walter Howells lived here for some years.
Left to right, back row Robert Davies, Joy Thorne, Susan Morris, Hazel Turner, Philip Rouse, Pauline Young, Alan Probert, Philip Skyrme, Roger Burgoyne, Michael Matthews, David Rouse.
Front row, Dawn Morgan, Keith Hodgson, Stephen Aubery, Maureen Preece, Christine Clark, Graham Evans, Ken Matthews, Christine Probert, Glyn Milward, Trevor Lloyd

climates and road conditions on the way. On its return to this country the bus had to be completely overhauled and it was eventually sold. Brian continued to work for the company for some years, driving through many countries and gathering a lot of experiences and memories, until he got married. He spent a short time in Hertford before returning to Eardisley and buying a house out of the village on the road to Almeley, and here he and Gillian brought up their family. For ten years Brian represented the Eardisley area on Leominster District Council, until this was abolished when Hereford became a unitary authority.

In later years Brian's interest turned to apple-growing and cider-making. After getting started with old machinery he decided to go to France and buy more modern equipment. This turned out to be yet another adventure and Brian told me of his and Gillian's trip. He borrowed a 4x4 Daihatsu from Mr Clive Davies, drove down with Gillian to Portsmouth and in the evening boarded a ferry boat to Caen. The ferry put to sea but as the night wore on a storm blew up: furniture and crockery were smashed in the bars and restaurants, vehicles were overturned on the cargo decks and the crossing eventually took more than twice as long as it should have done. Brian believes that the ship and the lives of her passengers were only saved by the prompt action of the captain in turning the vessel to face the full power of the wind. The crew did what they could for the comfort of the passengers, dispensing free drinks from the tea and coffee machines (which contained the only unbroken cups on board) but Gillian, like most people on board, was apprehensive about the outcome of the journey. Brian — typically — slept through it all. In the morning, when they disembarked at Caen, it was immediately evident from the broken trees and the damage to buildings how severe this storm had been. It was 16th October and the storm had been comparable with great storms in history. This was The Great Storm of 1987.

Arriving at last on dry land they drove off to buy the cider press. When they reached the address they had been given, however, the man Brian had been dealing with denied any knowledge of the press. But Brian was not beaten — off he went with Gillian, looking everywhere for a cider-press, driving into all sorts of farm premises, walking round farmyards and peering into barns. Eventually they came across the type of press Brian required and — I expect to Gillian's great relief as this had all taken several days — Brian struck a deal with its owner and they set off on the return journey.

They had a smooth crossing back to Portsmouth, arrived at Customs and Excise and then the complications began. What *was* the machine? the officials wanted to know — there was no record of any machine like it having been

Nowt at home in his garden in 2004, servicing the mighty machine he brought home from France (after using it to crush apples for cider — not, as Customs and Excise imagined, back in 1987, to pick apples!)

imported before. They had to know what it was in order to determine the basis for the import duty. After much discussion the verdict was that it was an apple-picking machine! The duty, they said, would be £100, but Brian could not just pay this direct to them; he had to use the services of a 'forwarding agent' to pay the Excise through a computer link. But the forwarding agent's fees would be a further £80 up-front.

In the early days of the Common Market VAT was still a grey area. After much further discussion the Department of Excise levied an account of £200 (which was non-returnable), which meant Brian had to visit the bank to draw extra cash. This the officials were prepared to accept, but by now it was lunch time and they closed the shutter. There would be another hour's delay.

The machine was eventually released from the Customs area but at this point the shipping company announced that they deemed it to be commercial freight and made a £50 surcharge. By now it had taken twelve hours to clear Customs, it was getting dark and there was still a slow journey ahead back to Eardisley — 165 miles on small roads and crossing Salisbury Plain. They made it home at long last and the cider-press proved to have been worth all the trouble, but Brian and Gillian often look back with mixed feelings on that trip to France as they drink their home-made cider.

When I first knew Eardisley Post Office it was run by Mrs Nellie Elizabeth Smith, who had been in charge there from 1918 and continued till 1950. She had a lot to attend to as she managed the telephone exchange as well (which was run off batteries in those days) and she had to send telegrams in Morse code. Mrs Smith had been married twice and lived in America for thirteen years before marrying Mr Smith and coming to live in Eardisley. From 1950 until 1965 it was run by Mr John Wallis Moulton. 'Jack' Moulton (as he was known in Eardisley) was active in village amateur dramatics and in Eardisley Fire Brigade, as well as many other things. When he died, on 28th September 1965, his wife, Mrs Margaret Mary Moulton took on the post office and ran it till 1971. The following year her daughter and son-in-law took over — Norah and Elwyn (my pal Nick) Nicholas. They ran the post office well and always joined in village activities. They were both well known and well liked in and around Eardisley. Elwyn died suddenly on 25th May 1996, aged 58. People in Eardisley still miss him and maybe this book will remind a lot of people how good a chap he was — 'my pal always'.

Eardisley post office was run from Hawthorn House by Mrs Heather Royle from February 1999 to 8th January 2002. At this point it moved to The New Strand — very convenient for a quick half pint. The new postmaster was Mr Ewan Cardwell, who opened for business on 10th January 2002. The post office was closed only for one day during the changeover. The hole in the wall at Hawthorn House where letters used to be posted was sealed up and a new red pillar box was erected at The New Strand.

Reg Jones pulling pints in The New Inn in the Sixties

Eardisley has two pubs at the top end of the village, opposite one another. The one is called The New Strand (at different times in the past it has been known as The Phoenix, The New Inn and The Mountie) and the other The Tram Inn.

The New Inn, as it was known when it was owned and run by Mr and Mrs Reg Jones, had a driveway to the back yard where the stables were and a lovely stone wall around a secluded private garden, with laurel hedges, flower beds and lawn. Built into the stonework were two or three metal bars where bicycles could be parked while the owner was having a drink or maybe checking bus times from the timetables on the notice boards. Mr Jones had served with the Welsh Guards and later with the Home Guard and the pub became the HQ for

New Inn crib team, 1950s. Left to right, Tom Penny, Bert Brown, Jimmy Marshall — my great uncle (my Granny's brother), Ernie Crump, Reg Jones, Ernie Brookes

128

the Home Guard in Eardisley. They usually came out from there quite high spirited and ready to take on Mr Hitler! In his younger days Mr Jones had played a lot of water polo and had been an excellent swimmer. During the thirty-five years he was landlord at The New Inn, he was very good to the village and especially to the British Legion. He was particularly good to village young-sters, often letting a room for them to go and play games — skittles or darts or something — and have a drink of pop and a packet of crisps — a real country landlord. He died in 1969.

The New Inn has changed hands (and names) a few times since then and it has seen changes. Different people have had different ideas and have done various things — for one thing, the lawn is no longer there as it has been built on.

When David and Kathleen Harvey took the pub over they renamed it The Mountie Inn. Then, when Mr and Mrs Ron Fitness bought it they renamed it The New Inn again. When Ron died the pub was sold to Mr and Mrs Baxter, and they sold it in 1995 to Mr and Mrs Robin and Ann Cardwell, who now run it under the name of The New Strand.

Since 1995 it has had quite a few alterations to it. An excellent eating area has been built onto the original building, where it is very pleasant to have a lunch or snack, at the same time watching the village with its passers-by or looking out onto the surrounding patio and play area. The eating area adjoins a shop selling gifts and books which is efficiently run by Mrs Briar Cardwell-Like — always a plea-sure to speak to, with her welcoming smile. Opened in 1996, the Strand book shop holds a stock of over 20,000 secondhand books of all sorts; after finding

Ewan Cardwell at the bar of The Strand in 2004

Briar Cardwell-Like in the dining room at The Strand in June 2003 with customers (Iris and Godfrey Skyrme, their son and daughter-in-law David and Laura, and their granddaughter). The windows behind look north-west, towards the Woodseaves road on the left and the Kington road on the right.

Briar Cardwell-Like in the book shop at The Strand in 2004

a book one likes it is very nice to be able to enjoy a snack or a meal, with a coffee or a beer. Of course the pub is still there at the hub, with its inviting ale, but the local post office is now run from there too. It all works very well. The various New Strand businesses are run by members of the family: Robin, Ann and Ewan Cardwell, and Briar Cardwell-Like. It is always a pleasure to meet them as they make one feel so welcome.

The Tram Inn opposite The New Strand is a black-and-white building built about 1500. When the horse-drawn tram was running they used to stable the horses at The Tram Inn stables. The tram, which was not for passengers but for goods, ran from Brecon to Eardisley and then on again to Kington, on track made in the foundries of Even & Vaughan of Blaenavon. Laying of the track was completed in 1818. The trucks, made of wood and metal, carried loads of one to two tons — coal brought down from Brecon, and stone, lime, or corn taken back up to Brecon; two horses went along the stoned area between the tracks pulling the trucks and these would be changed at various points. The Wharf at the bottom of the village had gates across the tramway and was closed each evening at dusk, as there was no traffic at night. A piece of the track, which was found by Mr Vampleux, who used to live in the village, was given to The Tram Inn in 1984 and is displayed there today.

The Tram Inn is very interesting. Melvyn and Claire Reynolds, who were landlords of The Tram in the early Nineties, have told me that they believe there is a ghost — a friendly ghost — at The Tram. They reckon they saw and heard the ghost themselves on several occasions. It was the ghost of a woman or a girl, perhaps Miss or Mrs Baird. (There was a landlord of The Tram in the 1930s called Baird.) Melvyn and Claire said the ghost was not at all frightening and

that one of their staff — Julie Standen — who lived in with them, saw her too.

I have seen a few different landlords at The Tram. Mr and Mrs Winston and Lorraine Wall arrived in Eardisley in October 1997, with their sons Matthew and Michael, as they had just bought The Tram Inn, and it was not long before they became popular with the locals and part of the community.

Peter Stockwell, then landlord, and an unknown customer, in about 1961, soon after Peter had had the new bar put into The Tram in about 1961. John (Butch) Preece is just visible in background.

They worked very hard at the business. The buildings were repaired where necessary, Tram Square was resurfaced, and all this gave a general uplift to the appearance of the pub. Win and Laurie also created four lovely boules pistes in the garden. The first piste was made in Spring 1998 and three more were added in Easter 2001. Most of the work was carried out by Jens Bryan and his contracting firm, who made an excellent

Carol Wilson and Paul Austin in the newly refurbished lounge bar at The Tram Inn in 2002

job of it and of the outdoor lighting. The garden of The Tram is now a very enjoyable place to go and compete, have a drink and meet people, and many exciting games have been played there.

Paul Austin and Carol Wilson took over The Tram in 2002 and altered and updated the lounge bar in November of that year. The last time it had been done before that was when Peter Stockwell put in a new bar in 1961.

People often stop and look round the village and take photos of the black-and-white buildings, then call and have a meal and a drink. Often the locals will meet some complete strangers on holiday and make conversation and in no time at all they feel part of the community and very welcome.

Another building that has been affected by change over the years is Eardisley rectory. My earliest memory of a parson was of the Rev. Sydney Osborne (we always called him Jerry), who regularly came to the school; of course the religious inspector would come as well, from time to time, to question the children and see if they knew their scripture. It was quite something to be told the inspector was visiting as my mates and I had so many other things in our minds at that time and usually found it quite hard to answer the questions. Mainly our thoughts were more on school time finishing so that we could get on with our main interests — riding horses or motorcycles or just repairing our bikes.

The rectory seemed a good place to be, with its lawns and chestnut trees; now and again Rev. Osborne would invite the children from the school over to a function with drinks on the lawn, or to pick up chestnuts. I remember the bowling green, where, as we grew older, we would go and have a game or watch

Bowls at the rectory in the late Forties or Fifties

older people play. With the sun going down it was a wonderful setting for a friendly chat.

In 1978 the Church acquired a more modern house in the village for the rector; the rectory and its garden were sold off and the bowling green and adjoining grounds became derelict.

In December 1998 Mr Paul King and his wife Mrs Susan King bought The Old Rectory, and more recently they also took on a tenancy of the bowling green area.

Bowls at the rectory. Left to right, Topsy Vaughan, Madeline Powell, Charlie Nicholas, Freda Lloyd (later Nicholas) and, actually bowling, our local cobbler, Dick Webb

Paul has put a lot of hard work into building repairs and he has also spent time and effort getting the bowling green area tidy again, which is good to see as it brings back a lot of happy memories.

For many years the rectory has been the home of Mrs Elwina Smith (usually known as Wina). Now 90, she takes care of her home and garden in a wonderful way (and always reminds me of the way things used to be, never appearing to tire but just getting on with life). Her garden is immaculately dug and planted each year — by herself — and she enjoys every minute as she goes about her daily jobs. What a wonderful character! There are many others too, still about in Eardisley, who, like Mrs Smith, are what I call 'of the old school', who just love to get on with life.

Elwina came to Eardisley in August 1954 and is often to be seen on a Sunday afternoon walking through the village to visit her sister Mrs Enid Hodgson in Hobby Lyons. Her husband, Mr Ernest Smith, who was a local lorry driver, died on 24th March 1994, aged 74 years, but Elwina, like so many others, keeps her chin up and a little smile, which is always nice to see. She worked for about fifteen years for Mother's Pride Bakery in Hereford until retiring at the age of 66. Like Mrs Marshall (who I wrote about earlier in this book), Elwina did war work in the munitions — and she too remembers the yellow hair! As Miss Jones then, Elwina worked at Rotherwas, in the ordnance factory, often working a night shift. She travelled to Hereford every day from Glasbury, where at the time she was living with her sister Mrs Alice Price, landlady of The Harp Inn, whose husband Will was away in the army. Mr Ernie Smith served with the Grenadier Guards during the war and served in many famous places including

Mrs Elwina Smith in her garden at The Old Rectory 2004

*Card commemorating a record peal of bells on
Sunday 11th August 1974*

Buckingham Palace and Windsor Castle and many places abroad until he was demobbed in Edinburgh. Like Wina, he loved his garden, and that's where he died, lighting his pipe in his garden shed at the rectory, Eardisley.

I was only nine months old when my family came to live at Ashcroft, at the side of Modello Works. I have learned since then that while we were living at The Wilkin our neighbours next door were the Jones family and they had a daughter called Evelyn. When I was born Evelyn was twelve years old, and, as she sometimes reminds me now, she came to see me very soon after my birth. Forty years later I found myself again neighbours with Evelyn. By this time she was married to Robert Hatcher and had two sons, Andrew and Stephen. Robert — Bob — Hatcher was keen on sport, he held several records for bell-ringing and he kept a very good garden. He also did a lot of work for the church. Sadly, he died on 11th February 1987 aged 62 years. We all miss him and his good work.

Evelyn (Ev, as she is usually known, though I still call her Mrs Hatcher) used to be a Girl Guide leader, she played hockey, she was involved with many activities, including amateur dramatics and has always kept herself busy with meetings and functions of all sorts. She has done, and still does, a lot of work for Eardisley, especially the church and the WI. She tells me — with a smile and a shrug of her shoulders — that some people call her Mrs *Tha*tcher ... She is a real asset to Eardisley and it is a pleasure and privilege to know her.

The Rev. Jennifer Pollock, the first lady parson in Eardisley, came here on 23rd May 1997. It was a wonderful experience to have a lady preacher. Jen, as she liked to be called, was often to be seen in summertime cycling through the village on her way to Almeley church, waving and acknowledging people. She was a picture to see, sitting upright, looking carefree, pedalling away — it reminded one of the way things used to be. I feel sure that on those rides to Almeley and the other parishes, with the hills in the distance and animals all around her, Jen would have been thinking 'What a wonderful world!' One day, Jen told me, while she was going from Eardisley to Almeley, as she was driving past Gypsy Hall, she had a surprise: a huge black cat-like animal (much bigger than an ordinary cat) crossed the road, just a few yards in front of her car. It crossed from her right to her left and disappeared up the drive of The Old

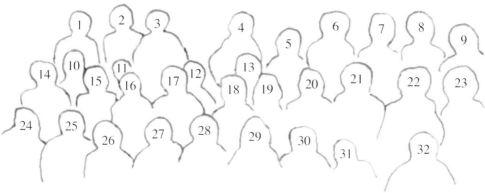

Eardisley WI 21st Birthday party, 1961. 1 Mrs Joe Taylor (Elsie), 2 Mrs Glen Probert (Joy), 3 Mrs Bill Button (Julia), 4 Mrs Trevor Turner (Brenda), 5 Mrs Ken Davies (Mary), 6 Miss Margaret Carter, 7 Miss Sheila Hamer, 8 Miss Pat Townsend, 9 Miss Rosemary Darling, 10 Mrs Frank King (Lucy),11 Miss Gertrude Gwatkin, 12 Mrs Norman Tebb, 13 Miss Enid Trumper, 14 Mrs Matthews, 15 Mrs Dick Griffin (Joan), 16 Mrs Denis Sharples (Edith Maud) — Jean's mother, 17 Mrs Harry Burgoyne (Josephine) 18 Mrs Ken Townsend (Mabel), 19 Mrs Frank Sandford (Gladys), 20 Mrs Reg Weale (Doris), 21 Mrs Jim Morgan (Eileen), 22 Mrs Tom Hicks (Mona), 23 Mrs Bob Hatcher (Ev), 24 Mrs Ron Chillingford, 25 Mrs Basil Thomas (May), 26 Mrs Dick Darling (May), 27 Miss Renee Townsend, 28 Mrs Frank Willford (May) — WI President, 29 Mrs Eva Cole, 30 Mrs Bas Wynne (Winifred), 31 Mrs Jack Page (Annie), 32 Mrs Francis Whittall (Alice)

The Rev. Jen Pollock and I had something in common not shared by many other people in the village. We both got a thrill from parachute jumping. On Saturday 27th September 2002 she did a sponsored parachute jump at Cirencester airfield to raise money for Eardisley school. I think Jen jumped only once but I know how much she enjoyed doing so. (An entry dated 21st September 2002, however, in the church's Names for Prayers book, in Jen's handwriting, suggests that she was not entirely relaxed at the prospect of the jump: 'Please pray for me as I make my parachute jump on Saturday.')

Quarry. 'It crossed the road quite casually', she said. (I'm not sure that we ever got to the bottom of that story, but I think there were several sightings of the animal, whatever it was.)

Jen was always the first to help where she could, visiting the sick and needy. I remember while doing a repair to my workshop, at home after recovering from an operation, I heard a voice behind me, a soft voice, say 'Hello, Brian. How are you getting on?' It was Jen and her visit was very unexpected, but it gave me a great lift.

I am so pleased to have taken the photo on 8th June 2004 showing Roger Prout, Catherine Galloway and our lovely parson, Jen, meeting in the churchyard

The Rev. Jen Pollock, Roger Prout and Catherine Galloway in Eardisley churchyard for the Transit of Venus, Tuesday 8th June 2004. Roger and Catherine have recently moved to Eardisley and are keen to be actively involved with village life. They are amateur astronomers (and good friends with Patrick Moore, who they hope will one day visit Eardisley). The viewing of the Transit of Venus was only the first of the many astonomical events they hope to be able to organize.

*Transit of Venus, Eardisley churchyard, Tuesday 8th June 2004. In the background,
Left to right, Catherine Galloway, Elizabeth Preece, Irene Higgs, Sonia Taylor. In the
foreground are children from Eardisley school. Transits of Venus occur in pairs eight
years apart. The first pair we know about happened in 1631 and 1639. We also know
of occurrences in 1761 and 1769, and in 1874 and 1882. The 2004 transit will be
paired with one in 2012 — but this will be visible only in Japan. The next time people
will be able to see this phenomenon anywhere on Earth will be in 2117 and 2125.*

of Eardisley church on a bright sunny day to watch the Transit of Venus. Jen is
looking happy in the picture, enjoying the historic event in which the school children and other villagers had the chance to see something they will probably
never be able to see again. She had a passion for history and her husband,
John, told me how excited she was that her name (as rector) was on the bell
that was cast for Almeley church recently — she knew her name would be there
for hundreds of years.

Not long after this photo was taken Jen became very ill and on 23rd
December 2004, at the early age of 53, she passed on. Words cannot describe
the way she is missed by us all. I feel sure she would have liked to read this book
about the goings-on in Eardisley, but, knowing Jen, I expect she already had a
good idea of what went on.

✻   ✻   ✻   ✻   ✻

When I was young there were still a lot of pony-and-traps about and the village seemed to have a wonderful atmosphere to it: people going in and out of the shops, the sounds of the animals and of course the smells — real country smells — harvest time, fruit picking — even now these smells can take one back in time. While the war was on and for a time afterwards people tended to 'make do and mend' things, and use things that were secondhand (or more). It seemed a great achievement to build yourself a bike from scrap parts, or maybe to get a few more miles out of your older brother's boots. I think we had a good child life in those days. We asked for nothing but we got a lot. As children then we seemed to be freer in some ways ... able to go out and do things ... camp and make dens. Looking back on it the time seems to have gone so quickly.

It is very different now. With the pace of everything and traffic of all sorts, we find it more difficult to stop in the village and spend time. But to me, and I am sure others, Eardisley still is a great place to be. It has a lot going for it with all the different activities and the country atmosphere. I am sure that people who have travelled far from the village, and for long periods, remember it. Many I know have returned so that they can finish their days here. It is just one of those places.

There is a song which goes 'a little bit of Heaven fell in the Irish Sea'. I think, a little bit of Heaven fell *here*, in Eardisley.

Index

Those entries in italics relate to illustrations.

Allan, Norman 123
      Shirley — see under Hales
Amos, Cecil 57, 50-51
Anning, Mrs Sheila 30
ARP 17
Arboyne House *78, 79, 82,* 116
Army Cadets 103, *103*
      Camp — see under Camp
Arrowsmith, Mrs 69
Ashby, Simon 73
Ashcroft (bungalow) 1, 54
Aubery, Stephen 125
Austin, Paul 132, *132*

Baird, Mrs 131
Bancroft, Mr 65
Bank House 42
Barker, Derry *47,* 49-50, *49,* 56-57, *56, 66,* 67-68, 87, *103,* 104
    PC George 50, 87, *87,* 88
    Hilda 87, 88
    Ronnie 56-57, *66,* 87
Barrett, Arthur 40, 50
Bateson, Mr Ernest 'Spud' 20-21, *21*
    Mrs Isobel *105*
Batts, Anne 9
    Fanny 9
Baxter family 94
    Queenie 94
Baxter, Mr & Mrs 129
Bedford, David *35*
    Hayley *37*
    John *37*
Bengry, Tom *17*
Bird's Pitch 65
Blanchard, Ann 19
    Mrs 17, 19
    'Pikey' 17, 19
Boat Inn, Whitney 25
Bounds, Bill *17,* 40
    Caroline 117
    Jossy 117
Bowen, Capt. 'Skip' 23-25, *23, 24*
    Jack *17*
    Muriel 23
Boyce, Lily 10
Bridge House 1, 6, *6*

Brierley, Mr William *43,* 44, 75-76, *76,* 110
    butcher's shop 75-76
British Legion 102
Bromage, Harry *17,* 58
Brook Cottage 36
Brook Farm *120*
Brookes, Dick 17, *84*
    Doreen *84*
    Dorothy *84*
    Miss Edith *2*
    Ernie *128*
    Miss Gertrude *102*
    Jack 110
    Jean *60*
    Mrs Rosa *2*
Brotherton, Jane *37*
    Jonathan *37*
Brown, Bert *128*
    Miss Edith *18,* 106
Bryan, Jens 132
Burgoyne, Amy 72
    Doug 73
    Doug junior 73
    Harry 1, 72, 73
    Mrs Josephine 4, *52, 136*
    Lynn 4
    Roger 73, *125*
    Tom 71-73
Burgoyne's garage 75
Busby, Miss 96
Button, Mrs Julia *136*
    PC 88

Camilla Cottage *4*
Camp, The 11
    as American Army base 11, 13, *13, 15*
    as POW camp 13
Cardwell, Ann 129, 131
    Ewan 127, *129,* 131
    Robin 129, 131
Cardwell-Like, Mrs Briar 129, *130,* 131
Carter, Charlie 16, *17,* 81-82
    John 106, *107*
    Kathleen 30
    Miss Margaret *136*
    Mel 30
    Mervyn 30

Richard *107*
Tom 26-30, *26*
Castle Close 3, *61*
Castle Farm 61-63
castle moat 59, 60-61, *61*
Charles, Anne *60*, *107*
John *107*
Ken *107*
Megan *60*, *107*
Mrs 36
Chillingford, Mrs Ron *136*
cider house, the *75*
Clark, Christine *125*
Eric 33-34, 81
Clematis Cottage 9, *9*
Cockerell, Dorothy *60*
Cole, Mrs Eva 136
Coudell, Robert 84
Cross Café, Winforton 88
Cruck House *81*
Crump, Ernie 7, *8*, 9-10, *9*, 36, *105*, *128*
Curzon Herrick Hall — see village hall

Dairy House 9
Darling, Kitty 6, 95-101, *98*
Mrs May 6, *6*, 7, *102*, *136*
Richard 1, *2*, 5-6, *6*
Miss Rosemary 7, *136*
Davies, Anne 37, 42
Barbara *60*
Bert *17*
Bill (of The Castle) *105*
Bobby *60*
Charlie *17*
Chris 85
Christine *60*
Clive 56, *107*
Denzil *60*
Derrick *60*
Ernie 'Child' *17*
Harold *12*
Mr and Mrs 61-63
Janet *74*
Jill 56, *107*
Mrs Mary *136*
Michael *3*
Myra 56, *107*
Mr and Mrs 'Napper' *5*, 74
Olive (née Morgan) 56, 63, *105*, *107*
Mrs 'Pecker' 1
Percy 'Barclay' *17*
Robert *125*
Walter *17*

Dawkins, Mr and Mrs *81*
Duke's, The 82
Dyke, Evan *17*

East View 3, 9, *18*
Edwards, WPC Lynne 88
Electric Sawmill, The 88
Evans, Doris 33
George *17*
Graham *125*

Faulkner, Ann *60*
Fellowes, John *105*
Field, The *121*
Fire Service 85-86
Station *85*, *119*
Firs, The 54
Fitness, Mr and Mrs Ron 129
flooding 119-122, *119*, *120*, *122*
Forest Fencing 14
Forester's Cottage 14, 22
Fox Supper, The 11, *12*
Franklin, Jean and Arthur 73
Franklin and Hodge 124

Gale, Mr 73
Mr Stan 36
Mrs Stella 35, 36, *37*
Galloway, Catherine 137, *137*, *138*
Goodwin, Andrew *37*
Ann 35
David 35
Susan 37
Tony *104*
Great Oak area 58, 59
School *60*
Gregg, Sergeant 47
Griffin, Mrs Joan *136*
Griffiths, Mrs Mary *102*, *105*
Rev. Reg *102*, *102*, 103, 104, *105*, 105
Grigg, Ethel *60*
Gwatkin, Miss Gertie 69, *136*
Miss Lilian 69, *102*

Hadley, Rill 71
Hales, Brenda 124
Colin *60*
Mrs Ellen *94*
Gerald 1, *2*, 6, *10*, *17*, 36, 44, 85, *85*, 88, *124*
Jack 13, *13*
J W & Co 123
John 1, 3, *3*, 99, 123

142

Leonard 94
Mrs Leonard *2*
Margaret 1, 4, *7*
Phyllis *13*
Shirley 1, 4, *4*, 6, *6*, *7*, *52*
Hall, Alan 116
Hamer, David *13*
Miss Sheila *136*
Hammond, Bert 75
Kenneth 81
Harvey, Dave 112, 129
Kath 115, 129
Hatcher, Andrew 135
Ev *52*, 135, *136*
Robert 135
Stephen *77*, 135
Hawthorn House 127
Hedgehog Hunt 112, 113-114
Herbert, PC 88
Hicks, Mrs Mona *136*
Tom 45
Higgs, Benny 124
Clara 1, *3*, *124*
Irene 138
Hill, Mrs *98*
Peter *103*
Hobby Lyons *80*
Hodgson, Mrs Enid 134
Keith *125*
Holme, The (boys' home) 9
Holmes, Gordon 54, *107*
Home Guard 16, *17*, 129
Howells, Esther 88
Peggy 88
Sam 93-94
Mr and Mrs Walter *125*
Walter 16, *17*, 85, 88, 94
Hughes, Bert 4, *5*

Ideal Bungalow 90
Institute, The 73

James, Mrs Bessie *102*
Jarrett, Desmond *43*, 56, 57, *107*
(?) Susan *37*
PC Edwin 87
Jenkins, Charlie *17*
Florence *60*
Mr 73
Tommy *60*
Tony *107*
Walter 33

Jones, Ann *60*
Anne (sister of Graham) *107*
Bernard *14*
Bill *46*
Brian 'Nowt' 16, 21, 26, 41, *46*, 47, *47*, 48, 53, 54, *54*, 55, *55*, 56, 67-68, 124-127, *126*
Dennis 45
Miss Doris *102*
Mrs Edith *102*
Gillian 125
Glyn 85, 103, 104
Graham 56, *56*, 59, *60*, *66*, 67-68, *107*
Jack *17*
John 42
Marian *107*
Marjorie *46*
Nesta *107*
Olive *60*
Oliver *17*, 35, 36, 38, *38*, *46*
Reg *17*, 112, 128, *128*, 129
Mrs Rose *42*, *102*
Sid *17*, 85, 94
Trevor 'Popper' *43*, *55*, 57-58
Vic 45
Jones's Garage 11, *14*, 38-39
breakdown van *43*, 44
steam engine 39-42
Jubilee bungalows 88

King, Miss Lucy *136*
Paul and Susan 133
Roy 113
Kite, Fred *2*, *17*
Knapp House 115
Knights, David *43*, *60*
Robert *43*, *103*

Ladies' Football Team *52*
Lady Arbour Farm *62*
Lane, Diane *35*
Tim *35*
Tony and Pat 75
Langford, Mr & Mrs *98*, *121*
Jack *17*
Larke, Michael *116*
laundry 69
Layton, Brenda *107*
Jeanette *107*
Olwen *107*
Peggy *107*
Leake, Miss Elizabeth May 82-83, *82*
Harriet 82

Lewis, Jill and Leonard 114, *114*
    Jim *116*
    Trevor *54*
Llewellyn, David *35*
    Jenny *35*
    William *35*
Lloyd, Brynis *49, 60*
    Carmen and Peggy 58
    Esau *60*
    Freda *133*
    Grace *60*
    Joy *49*
    Sam *60*
    Trevor *125*

Malt House, The 124
March House 124
Marshall, Becky *80*
    Jim *80, 128*
    Mrs Hannah Elizabeth 31-32
Matthews, Colin *35*
    Ken *125*
    Michael *125*
    Mrs *136*
McLeod-Black, Alexander *116*
Merrick, Lisa *35*
Mifflin, Sam *17*
Miller, Dr 16
Milward, George 90, *91*
    Glyn *125*
    Jack 88-92, *90, 91, 92*
    James *89*
    Mrs 69
    Martha 88, 91-92
    Mary 89, *89*
Modello Works (Garage) 1, *2*, 4, 5, 7-8, *10*,
        33-37, *34*, 86, 123, 124
    bus service 5, 34, *34*
    school car service 34-35, *35*
    taxi service 36-37
Morgan, Cyril 45
    David 109
    Dawn *125*
    Edgar *17*, 60, 62
    Mrs Eileen *136*
    Frank *17*, 83
    George 14, *83*
        wood mill 14, *83*
    Jim 115-118, *116, 117*
        and 'horned' rabbit *117*
    'Jim' (Cyril) 70, 115
    Muriel 70-71, *70*

    Thelma *70, 107*
    Tom and Maggie Louise 70
    Wilfred *17*, 70-71, *70*
Morgan's Shop 70-71, *70*
Morris, Mrs Edith *105*
    James 16, 109, *109*
    John *17*
    Mr 65
    Mrs, the Folly 88
    Susan *125*
Morrish, Mr 79
Moulton, Frank 47, 56, 105-108
    Jack 85, 88, 105, 127
    Margaret Mary 127
    Norah 105
    Mrs Peggy *102*, 105
    Stuart 105
Mountie, The, see New Strand
Murrell, Bill 105

Nash, Noreena *107*
Needes, Keith 49, *50, 66, 111*
New Inn, see New Strand
New Strand 113-114, 127, 128-131, *129, 130*
Newman's Place 58
Nicholas, Billy 85, 86
    Charlie *133*
    Elwyn 'Nick' 16, *43*, 53, *54, 55*, 56,
        67-68, 93, *104*, 110-112, *111*, 127
    Mrs Freda *102*
    Norah *52, 111*, 127
    Wlliam and Florence 53
Northway 115
Nowt — see Jones, Brian

Old House, The 69
Olde House, Ye 73
Orchardville 75
Osborne, Rev. Sydney 132

Page, Mrs Alice *102*
    Mrs Annie 8, *98, 101, 102, 136*
Parker, Mrs Phyllis *12*
Parry, Edward *12*
    Herbert *12*
    Miss 21
    Muriel 105
Payne, Doreen *52*, 94, 95
Penny, Tom *128*
Peppi the donkey 114-115, *114*
Philpotts, Mrs Bertha 102
Plumstead, Humphrey 55, 65, 100
    Prue 106, *107*

144

Pollock, Rev. Jen 135, 137-138, *137*
    John 138
Porter, Alderman W D *85*
Post Office 127
Povey, Mrs Joan *105*
Povey's butcher's shop 80, 82
Powell, David(s) *19*, 49, 109, 110-112
    John 49
    Madeline *18*, *105*, *133*
    Margaret *19*
    Percy *19*
Powell's Farm 3
Preece, Mrs Angeline *37*
    Ella *3*
    Elizabeth *138*
    Frank *40*
    John 11, *12*
    Maureen *125*
    Peter 109, 124
    Sam *12*
Price, Eddie 40
    Lewis *17*
Prideaux, Ewart 22
    Geoff 22
    Jack *17*
Prime, Joy 96
Pritchard, Miss Freda *105*
    George 11, *12*
Probert, Alan *125*
    Christine *125*
    Mrs Joy *136*
    Stewart *116*
Prosser, Arthur 85
    Mrs Arthur 113
    Celia 96
Prout, Roger 137, *137*

Radziejowski, Philip 116, *116*
railway carriages 4-5, *5*, 19, 74
    station 83-84
Rawlins, Brian *60*
Raymond, Debbie *35*
    Robert *37*
    Tony *37*
rectory, the 132, *133*, 134
    bowling green 132, *133*
Reynolds, Melvyn and Claire 131
riding 14, 22, 55
Rouse, David 125
    Philip 125
Rowlatt, PC Bill 88, 113
Royle, Mrs Heather 127

Sandford, Mrs Gladys *136*
school, the *20*
    days 19-22
scouts 104
Sharples, Mrs Edith Maud 136
Sherwood, Shân 74
Skyrme, David *130*
    Godfrey *17*, *130*
    Iris *130*
    Laura *130*
    Philip *125*
Smith, Miss Annie *102*
    Beryl 37
    Derek 37
    Edna *105*
    Elwina 134-135, *134*
    Ernest 134-135
    H.W. & Son *75*
    Isabel *105*
    Mandy *37*
    Miss Nellie Elizabeth 127
Smythe, Dr Edward *12*
Southgate, Miss Ethel *102*
Southway *125*
Spearman, Mr 75
Sports and carnivals 52, *52*, 83, 110, 115
Stampedes 112-113, *112*
Standen, Julie 131
Stephens, Gwyn *17*
    Tom 35, 36
    Mr and Mrs V 22
Steptoe, Donald 106
Stockwell, Peter *131*
Stoneleigh 69
Stratton, Miss 21
Sun Inn, Winforton 11

Tauber, Edwin 14
    Irene 14
    Isaac 13-14
Taylor, Mrs Elsie *52*, *136*
    Ronald *17*
    Sonia 82, *138*
Tebb, Mrs Norman *136*
Tennis Club 9, *105*
Thames Timber 14
Thomas, Mr A V 85
    Byron 22
    Mrs May 69, *136*
    Roy 43-44, *43*, 47, 48, *55*, 67-68
Thorne, Joy *125*
timber mills 14, 88

Tippins, Mrs Alice *102*
Tomlinson, Mrs Edith *107*
Tong, Mrs *102*
Townsend, Ken 14-16, 42, 52, 85, 86
    Mrs Mabel *52, 136*
    Miss Pat *52, 136*
    Miss Renee *136*
Tram Inn 11, *12, 78*, 114-115, *114, 122*, 131-132, *131*
    ghost 131
Tram Square *78, 79*
Triffitt, Mrs Marian *107*
Triffitt's 73
Trumper, Miss Enid 88, *136*
    Miss Gertrude *102*
    Miss Lil *102*
Turner, Mrs Brenda *102, 136*
    Hazel *125*

Vallender, Betty *60, 107*
    Doreen *60*
    Mrs Nancy *102*
Vampleux, Mr 131
Vaughan, Topsy *133*
Venus, Transit of 137-138, *137, 138*
village hall 65, 73
    film nights at 65

Wall, Winston and Lorraine 131-132
Weale, Mrs Doris *136*
Wearing, George 33
Webb, Dick, cobbler's shop 77-78, *77*, 79, *133*
    Mr and Mrs Rowland 73, 104, 105

wedding pranks 37-38
Wharf, The 53, 94
White House, The 19, 79
Whittall, Mrs Alice *136*
    David *60*
    John *60*
    Kathleen *60*
    Robert *15*
WI *136*
Wilding, Allen 124
Wilkin, The 1
Willford, Mrs May *52, 136*
Williams, Mrs Beatrice *2*
    Bill *5*
    Mrs H *102*
    Jim 35-36, *37*
    Owen *17*
Wilson, Carol 132, *132*
    Philip 117
Wolsey, Miss Kathleen *18*
Wood, Andy 26
    Ann 26, *52*
    Elizabeth 26, *52*
    Rodney 26, *26*
    Steve 26
Wooton Farm 22
Wynne, Robert 1, 11, *12*, 80-81
    Mrs Winifred *136*

Yare, Mr 65
Young, Pauline *125*